BUSINESS IN THE REAL WORLD

ELENA S. LIM

For students and aspiring entrepreneurs.

There are no barriers to your dreams except yourself.

CONTENTS

"After a worldwide search, Elena Lim is the only Filipino industrialist included in World*business* Magazine's list of *50 WORLD-CLASS EXECUTIVES*.

"More than her financial success, Elena has earned recognition for her pioneering edge — each of her business ventures is a story of entrepreneurship, creative management, reformation both in private business and government and the drive for global competitiveness in exports.

"It is because of these accomplishments that her alma mater has chosen her the Most Outstanding Alumna on the school's golden anniversary and conferred on her the degree of Doctor of Humanities, *honoris causa*.

"This book only proves that we have not really honored her — she honors us."

P. O. DOMINGO
Chairman of the Board
and President
University of the East

66 It is entrepreneurs like Elena Lim who are bringing progress and prosperity to the country. Elena Lim looked inwardly and found duty; she looked outwardly and just found duty became aspiration. Finally, she looked upward and found faith and I mean faith in the Filipino.

"Entrepreneurship and good management of limited resources are found in all her business experiences. The stories in this book are inspiring, courageous, revealing, and instructional. They could change your attitude, your way of doing things, and even your life."

ALEJANDRO R. ROCES
Chairman
Philippine Centennial
Foundation

66 Elena Lim's energy is contagious — anyone who knows her well will sooner or later be influenced by this dynamo of a woman! She has been involved in many, many pioneering economic efforts that have been of benefit to the Philippines, creating thousands of jobs, developing new skills for the country, and earning much needed foreign exchange. From TV sets to tiger prawns to people's car to industrial estates — and to the first major plant in the former Clark Air Base when the ashes from Mt. Pinatubo were still worrying less courageous entrepreneurs.

"One often wonders how a small lady (less than five feet tall) can do so much. But watch her, as I have, on trips with Philippine Presidents attracting investments from abroad and you are soon infected by her enthusiasm. Nothing is impossible for Elena — her strong determination to achieve her objectives is legendary! By now competitors have learned never to underestimate her. While building a business empire, Elena has greatly contributed to the economic growth of the Philippines and the economic well-being of its people.

"This book on her business experiences and insights is surely among her most priceless contributions — especially for aspiring entrepreneurs!"

WASHINGTON SYCIP
Founder
The SGV Group

66 Elena Lim's book is inspiring, a must for would-be and budding entrepreneurs so they can learn from her experiences as a mega-entrepreneur.

"From the case studies on her experiences, entrepreneurs can learn how to prevent potential problems and pitfalls. She also shows the way to overcoming barriers when they occur."

FELIPE B. ALFONSO
President, Asian Institute
of Management
Chairman, Manila Electric
Company

FOREWORD

I remember a poem I used to teach my high school students.

Invictus

Out of the night that covers me,
  Black as the pit from pole to pole,
I thank whatever gods there be
  For my unconquerable soul.

In the fell clutch of circumstance
  I have not winced nor cried aloud.
Under the bludgeonings of chance
  My head is bloody, but unbowed.

Beyond this space of wrath and tears
  Looms but the Horror of the shade,
And yet the menace of the years
  Finds and shall find me unafraid.

It matters not how strait the gate,
  How charged with punishments the scroll,
I am the master of my fate:
  I am the captain of my soul.

- William Ernest Henley

It has been a long time — more than 40 years — since then. The teacher became an entrepreneur. My students . . . I wonder what they have become.

I remember the poem because I have written this book for much the same reason I tried, long ago, to teach the poem well.

It is to help people realize that all problems are surmountable. Even the problem of poverty. You just have to have enough faith in God and yourself.

Through this book, I hope to help give hope. Especially to those who are now going through what I went through.

I even sold tomatoes in the public market of Leyte. I married Joseph Lim and we had to start our business from rock bottom — no economic or political connections, with only very little money from hard-earned savings, virtually nothing but our willingness to work hard and courage to face all adversities. If my husband and I could do it, of course, you can do it too.

This book contains more than forty years worth of business experiences and insights. The immense problems I faced and how I solved them without compromising fundamental principles. The successes and the disappointments. The heartaches and headaches, as well as the joys.

It also contains clear, solid proof that the Filipino is capable of world-class entrepreneurship. I have always taken pride that my companies are Filipino-owned, Filipino-managed, Filipino-staffed — and in the Philippine consumer electronics industry, we have competed against the multinationals and we are No. 1. At a time when Filipinos are often seen as a lesser people, we must take every opportunity to prove to the world that the Filipino is second to none. We must make every Filipino proud of being a Filipino.

I hope this book will give you, dear reader, practical lessons on how to succeed in entrepreneurship. That it inspires you to become an entrepreneur — to create, to innovate, to endure, to persist in your vision to become a leader in any activity of your life.

Above all, to keep your soul intact in the process.

ACKNOWLEDGMENTS

First acquaintances often tell me, "You must be lucky . . . you must have the Midas touch to make money in all your companies."

Many friends say, "How do you manage so many companies and still make a happy family? How were you able to raise all your children to become accomplished business executives? How could you find time to write this book?"

To both friends and acquaintances, I say: No one person does all these things you attribute to me. I could not have attained them without God's blessings and the wonderful support and teamwork of my husband, children, managers and employees. I do not have the Midas touch. This is a myth.

As to writing this book, I am lucky indeed in having a small group of dedicated friends who helped me transform my experiences into this small book of case studies of some of my companies.

Whenever I get an inspiration and feel like sharing my experiences in doing business in my country, I simply jot down from memory events that were both thorns and joys in my entrepreneurial journey.

This exercise has led to many hundreds of handwritten pages. I do not have staff to do much research because these stories come from my personal experiences and encounters with the varied sectors of our society.

It was an absolute pleasure working with my friends. Without them, there was no way I could have finished this book.

I refer to Nonong Tubio, a man with a deep sense of humanity and an expert in business finance and organization, who helped in the conceptualization, data-verification, and general organization of this book.

Lito Macachor, educator and finance executive whose values lie beyond numbers. He assisted in editing the book.

Mimi Palma Albaladejo, a wonderful friend who edited many case studies and whose devotion to her Christ-centered faith heightened my sense of compassion and spirituality.

Raymond Lim Toledo, head of Pacific Rim Advertising, who describes himself as a struggling writer and entrepreneur. He worked most seriously on this project without losing mind, wit, and humor, and took care of overall editing, layout, and printing.

Their wonderful support brought much joy to me during the hectic months devoted to this book.

I am grateful to them all for their help — especially for the enthusiasm, excitement, and excellent companionship during the rush period.

To all who took time to read and endorse this book: P.O. Domingo, Chairman and President of the University of the East; Alejandro R. Roces, Chairman of the Philippine Centennial Foundation; Washington Sycip, Founder of the SGV Group; Felipe B. Alfonso, President of the Asian Institute of Management and Chairman of the Manila Electric Company. I am in their debt.

To you, dear reader. You are the reason for this book's being.

I pray God that you all be filled with His graces, that your lives be happy and noble.

Chapter One

MY STORY

The simplest questions,

it is said, are the most profound. Who are you? How are you? Where are you from? Where are you going? What do you want? Why?

This book is more a collection of stories or, more technically, "case studies," about some of my business experiences than it is my life's story (I still have to write my autobiography). But their basic context is my life, and I am sure seeing them in proper context will help the reader see their nuances better. As an astute writer put it, "Text without context is pretext."

My initial answers, then, to these simplest questions.

Why I am less than five feet tall,

I often teased my late mother, must be due to all the water-fetching I did as a young girl.

I come from the poor province of Leyte. I was orphaned by my father when I was only three years old.

My mother, Evelyn Redobla Sen, was just turning 30 then, and on her shoulders fell the burden of raising six children. There was Lucy, the eldest, followed by Pablo, Pedro, Teresa, myself, and Antonio.

We eked out a living in Tacloban, Leyte, by making and selling shoes and slippers.

I was often described as easy-going and more devoted to telling jokes than hitting the books, although I was an honor student in both elementary and high school. Nevertheless, I was not able to escape from my mother's training in frugality and hard work, especially after father died.

I was not spared from household chores like washing and ironing clothes, cleaning the house, and cooking.

My mother even made me and my sister fetch water from the market so we could cook meals, launder clothes, and bathe.

We fetched water by using kerosene cans which we slung from our shoulders using a thick bamboo stick. Because I was only nine years old and my sister, ten years old at the time, we had a hard time carrying those cans of water from the marketplace to our house. We really found water-fetching to be a hard and arduous task — so much so that we had to resort to putting pillows on our shoulders to cushion our shoulders from the hard bamboo.

In later years, I would joke to my mother that perhaps my fetching heavy loads of water over long distances contributed to my rather stunted growth. After all, my mother was quite tall for a Filipina at five-feet-four inches, while until now I do not even clear five feet.

My mother was addressed with deference as *"maestra"* by everyone who knew her. It has been a long time since she died, but if she could only see me now, she would surely give me her nod of approval. Perhaps she would also give herself a pat on the back, too, because her naughtiest child, Elena, is finally devoting her boundless energy to something more worthwhile than climbing the nearby mountains in the town (now city) of Tacloban in her spare time.

My credo in the worth of work reflects the legacy left me by my mother. To share what I have for the success of others has been a lifelong objective. This trait of sharing belongs to my mother who believed that compassion expressed sincerely to every man, woman, and child bestows a calmer and collected personality to the giver. To me, this is the essence of accomplishment in life.

I was a bill collector

too when I was young. I can still remember my experience in collecting from a well-to do Spanish family in town who got three pairs of shoes from us on credit.

Every morning, on my way to school, I would pass by their house and knock. I would then say that I had come to collect the payment for the shoes, and I would be told: *"Malas! Buisit an nagsusukot san aga tungod san nasirang pala an adlao. Buwelta ka na la."* (It is bad luck to collect in the morning because the sun is just rising. Come back later.)

At noon, I would pass by the house again on the way home from school, and I would be told: "You're disturbing our lunch" or "siesta," whichever was fit.

When I would come in the late afternoon or early evening, after doing my household chores, I would be told: "It is bad luck to pay at night, because the sun is setting."

But I persisted in coming back to collect, so that eventually the pairs of shoes were fully paid for.

Experiences like this made me realize, at an early age, how hard it is to be an entrepreneur. One has to be tolerant, tenacious, and never giving up amidst trials.

Today, the challenge is even greater. Many entrepreneurs encounter clients who delay payments many months beyond the agreed period. It's not surprising to hear many companies going bankrupt because they can't get their receivables on time. Some people say the hardest part in a transaction is the collection.

What many businessmen don't seem to realize is that your business is only as good as your integrity which, among others, means paying your obligations on time. The lesson here is that you must keep your reputation as an honorable person because the foundation of business is trust.

Flash Gordon, Ming the Sorcerer,

Superman, Mandrake the Magician, the Lone Ranger, Tarzan, Rin Tin Tin, and Dick Tracy are living characters in my memory.

They were among my first business partners.

I first met them through a very rich classmate whose sister owned comic books which were promptly thrown away after one or two readings. Since the comic books were just rotting in a corner of my classmate's house, I asked if I could have them.

They were given to me and that started my comic books business. A classic example of how one's garbage can be another's treasure.

I rented the comic books out to other children for a few centavos. As a bonus for my numerous customers, mostly children, especially for our poor neighbors who couldn't understand English, I gave dramatic verbal translations in *Waray*, the local dialect, complete with sound effects and live action. My captive (and paying!) audience inspired me with their rapt attention and sincere applause. It felt good to be giving them their money's worth. What with reading and performing the same comic books over and over, I soon knew them by heart. And despite the years, they have stayed there. Little did I realize then that it was my first experience with multi-media presentations.

Work hard. Play fair. Be decent.

These values were drilled into us by our mother.

Thus, aside from selling shoes and slippers in our tiny shop, I was also involved in selling tomatoes in the public market. And right after World War II, I was a waitress in our small and nameless restaurant.

The fact that it was the only restaurant in Tacloban during that time was another proof of my mother's business foresight. At that time, many battle-weary GIs longed for good food and whiskey. My mother opted for good food (our neighbors opted for whiskey, not necessarily good).

For five dollars, we served very tasty fried chicken and *Chow Mien*. Often, there was a long queue and I believe it was due to our philosophy of serving good food at fair prices. I still remember my beautiful sister being called "Princess" by homesick marines, seabees, and navy sailors.

We almost died

in a fire that reduced to ashes our house in Tacloban. This happened about two years after the end of World War II. We also lost most of our belongings in that fire. My mother then decided that we should move to Manila. By then, I had almost finished high school.

I became a kindergarten teacher

at a small Chinese school in Manila. I remember that I would come in early each day because I had to ask my co-teachers the Chinese translations of English words I would be teaching my student that day. For example, in order to teach my students the word "dog," I had to tell them that the Chinese word for it is *"kao."* But I also learned that Chinese is such a difficult language that one has to be very careful with pronunciation because the meaning might be changed. My students and co-teachers used to laugh at me because I would be murdering the Chinese language. What with my heavy *Waray-waray* accent which was the dialect I was most comfortable with then.

I was able to go to night school to pursue my degree in Education because of this first job, as well as the others that followed — that of a sales clerk at an American PX store, and that of a high school teacher teaching English and History.

People are often surprised when they learn that before I became an entrepreneur, I was a teacher.

Looking back, I count my years in the academe among my happiest.

I also worked as a tutor in English

to earn more, and it was through my tutoring sessions that I met the man whose remarkably sharp business acumen bore the promise of a fruitful and harmonious complement to my own developing talents on that side of life.

What really attracted me to him, however, had nothing to do with any dream about business. My heart and mind were drawn to his innate character of simplicity, kindness, compassion, and a kindred feeling for people.

To this day, I have yet to hear my husband mention one name of a person whom he dislikes. He lives by the conviction that all persons are created good and that if anyone turns out to be bad afterwards, it is not due to his natural bent. Rather, it is the result of a lack of opportunity to be guided and cared for by someone who can bring out the goodness within that person. He used to tell me: "Never say anything negative about anyone. It is better not to say anything at all if you cannot say anything nice and true about that person."

Thus, when he proposed a partnership of a lifetime, I could not say "No" but shyly nodded "Yes."

His name is Joseph Lim, and he is a Filipino who worked in a glass store and rose from the ranks to become its sales manager.

We started our business from rock bottom. We did not have economic and political strength. It was a slow, arduous, and painful climb for us in business.

My only strength and tools during those difficult times were the values my mother taught me. I did not shun hard work and manual labor. I developed an inner strength and a gutsy stomach to take falls, disappointments, and failures.

Joseph and I

embarked on wholesaling and importing a variety of products such as all kinds of sheet glass, synthetic resins, and canned goods. By the time we had clinched the exclusive distributorship and manufacturing rights of the world-famous Sony electronic products in the Philippines, we had racked up between us an array of modestly successful business ventures.

At the same time, we did not allow ourselves to be outdone by our businesses. We managed to have four children: Susan, David, Jason, and Vincent. By God's grace, I also gained a Bachelor of Arts degree in Education, a Master's degree in English, sans thesis, two years of Medicine (my childhood dream was to become a doctor but poverty stood in the way), and, finally, a Bachelor of Law degree which culminated in my passing the bar exams.

All these academic degrees were earned at night schools since my day time was devoted to work and to running the family.

The small college where I got my bachelor's degree in Education is no longer existing today. I guess it existed mainly to cater to working students who could only attend evening school.

My alma mater in my law degree is the University of the East, a great institution known for its business and law courses. Its graduates are often among the topnotchers in the government's bar, as well as in the examinations for Certified Public Accountants (CPAs).

What I am today

and what I have achieved in my almost four decades in business could not have been done through wishful thinking and inaction.

Today, I am proud and happy to say that the companies I am associated with came not only from hard work but are also anchored on my strong faith in our country and people. I have made the Filipino the focus of my vision. Allow me to cite some examples.

Solid Corporation

has the distinct honor of being the Exclusive Manufacturer of Sony products in the Philippines (since 1971) while retaining Filipino management and workforce.

Our manufacturing activities for Sony have resulted in the birth of ancillary activities that include distributing, promoting, marketing, and servicing all Sony products throughout the country. It was focused work which committed not only ourselves, the whole work complement, but more importantly, got all my children enthusiastically contributing to the growth of Sony in the country. This they did by their own accord and I am grateful for this blessing because it brought the family closer together and the bond has grown stronger through the years.

We have made Sony No. 1 in the domestic market. We have also pioneered in the export of TV monitors, black-and-white TV, and cassette recorders. Solid Corporation is a shining example of a Filipino corporation succeeding in a field dominated by multinationals. It has continually belied the myth that only multinational companies can succeed in this industry.

AA Export

and Import Corporation pioneered in the export and marketing of black tiger prawn.

At first, the Japanese did not like the black tiger prawn because of its color. I had to personally go to Japan and demonstrate that the black tiger, when cooked, would turn into a deliciously reddish color. Today, because of Filipino ingenuity, it is accepted not only in Japan but all over the world.

We hardly imagined that it would grow into an industry that would create jobs in the countryside, improve the lives of Filipino fishermen and farmers, and contribute one quarter of US$1 billion annually to the country's export revenue.

In 1984 when our economy was in shambles and "Jobo Bills" (Treasury Bills named after then Central Bank Governor Jose "Jobo" Fernandez) of the Central Bank were peddled at 45% interest, I decided to put up a P20 million prawn processing plant in Bacolod, when nobody had faith in Negros Occidental due to the collapse of the sugar industry.

I patiently waited for two years before any prawns from growers could be processed to serve as start-up production for our plant. Inspired by our vision, the Negrenses took the challenge and prawn exports became a major industry. While it has taken a downturn in the past four years, I am happy to report that it is again on the upswing, and we are heading its resurgence with more intensive research and development related to the prevention of prawn diseases and maintenance of good health practices.

If business were to exist only to earn profits, it would have been much easier to put the P20 million in Jobo Bills and I would have doubled my money in a short time. However, stocks and Jobo Bills pale against my trust in the Filipinos. My plant created hundreds of jobs, earned foreign exchange, increased revenues for both local and national government, and upheld the Filipino. This is more than money . . . It is faith, hope, vision, and mission.

The People's Car
was espoused by Columbian Autocar Corporation because I felt that Filipinos deserve a less expensive mode of transportation than what was being offered at the time by the three big Japanese-led car manufacturers.

We introduced the Kia Pride, the first-ever people's car brand in the market. Until then only three Japanese car brands could be seen on the streets. I saw the unfairness of this and challenged the government to change their policy. It took more than a year to fight this cause before change finally came. I thank God for using me as His tool to initiate the change.

The Laguna
International Industrial Park (LIIP), our joint-venture industrial estate development company, is another example of a change process.

This 117-hectare industrial estate features facilities that investors would look for in a business site: wide paved roads, strong water supply, modern telecommunication facilities, even the Biñan interchange and road network worth one-hundred-forty-million pesos (P140 M) which we donated to the Philippine government. Today, every vehicle that passes this infrastructure pays P6.50 to the Toll Regulatory Board (TRB) and this includes my manufacturing companies which operate in the estate. With so many other factories using this facility, I'm sure the toll collection is a hefty contribution to government.

We began development for the LIIP in early 1990, at a time when no businessman would seriously think about investing in the Philippines as this was immediately after the December 1989 coup. We had the full consent of the farmers and the government, but still the process took more than two years of hard work because of countless problems.

The good thing, though, is that the project is now paying off: the place has been totally sold out but the inquiries from foreign investors who want to build their factories at LIIP still keep coming. What truly makes me happy is that these investments are creating thousands of new jobs for Filipinos.

Each factory we established

is a testimony to the Filipino spirit to strive and to seek for a better tomorrow. It symbolizes faith and the willingness to sacrifice. It becomes a center for many young Filipinos to work together, to care not only for good work but for one another. To be together to speak the brotherhood language. Yes, a symbol of a bond with a unity of dreams, hopes, and vision.

Do you still have dreams?

Are there still challenges that excite you? Often I am asked these questions.

Yes, I still have dreams.

I dream of exporting goods, not people.

I dream of that day when we Filipinos will be exporting more of our goods and services and less of our most precious resource, our people.

It always pains me to think of our overseas contract workers — our fathers or mothers, husbands or wives, brothers or sisters — who suffer loneliness and deprivation just to earn a little more for their families. We should strive to provide enough working opportunities so that Filipinos need not go abroad to earn a living.

I dream of happy Filipino children.

I dream of the day when there will be no more "street children." That we have street children, denied of everything that every child should have, is perhaps our biggest crime as a people. I dream of the day when every child can live in a safe and decent home, with enough love, enough food, enough education to grow up and become a happy and productive human being.

I dream

that by the third millenium, the Philippines can emerge as a new economic dragon and be accorded full respect and confidence among the nations on planet Earth.

I dream that our leaders and public officials be richly endowed with nobility to give exemplary public service, even at great personal sacrifice.

I dream of the empowerment of our people to take the initiative to actively work with government to remove the latter's ineptitude and conspicuous failures for the past decades. Yes, tons of regulatory red tape and oftentimes mindless layers of bureaucratic rules suffocate and kill the entrepreneurial spirit to get things done.

I dream of many thousands of Filipinos as successful entrepreneurs providing millions of jobs to our people.

I dream of our people with happy homes, good health and education, fortified with strong moral values and living in environmentally friendly surroundings.

I dream of us caring for each other.

I dream of our children taking their places in society and building a much better world than the one we leave them.

I remember

a conversation I had with a young man, a graduate of the University of the Philippines (UP), the nation's premiere state university.

UP students are often called *"Iskolar ng Bayan"* ("Scholars of the People") because at least 2/3 of the cost of their top quality education is shouldered by taxes from the Filipino people.

Much is therefore expected from every UP graduate in terms of service to their fellow-Filipinos. For my young friend, this was no empty rhetoric. He truly wanted to repay his debt of gratitude by using what he had learned in school to improve the lives of his people, especially the poor.

He expressed to me his anger at the manner traditional politicians waste public resources through corruption coupled with incompetence. He noted that, indeed, politics is too important to be left to politicians.

"So why don't you run for public office?" I asked. "You are exactly the kind of public servant the nation needs now."

He laughed bitterly. "I don't even have enough money to run for *barangay* councilor (the lowest elective position at the village level). Nor do I have any 'connections'."

My young friend noted the urgent need to change the political structure to make it more democratic and truly oriented to a new mode of political leaders bereft of every vestige of the "trapo" (Filipino colloquialism for "traditional politican"; in Pilipino, the word "trapo" also means "dirty rag").

He continued: "A new social order should evolve to give more representation and say to as wide a spectrum of society as possible. No person or family should have political power beyond one term. There must be room for other equally capable Filipinos.

"This may sound alien to our democracy, Filipino style, which languishes in the empty rhetoric of `it's the will of the people . . . the people have spoken,' etcetera. The truth is the people have no choice. The system perpetuates the few. The system has no room for transfer of power to the many.

"There must be a Philippines in the future where we do not see the same names for the past 50 years in the seats of political power. It's like a *rigodon* (traditional dance where various couples change partners; the dance ends with the original partners being paired again) where the powerful families take turns in occupying and perpetuating their positions.

"Just look at the list. Someone should make a list and see how the *rigodon* comes out. It's *lola* (grandmother), *lolo* (grandfather), *tatay* (father), *nanay* (mother), *tiyo* (uncle), *tiya* (aunt), *kapatid* (brother/sister), *pamangkin* (nephew/ niece), *apo* (grandchild), etc., etc.. This is defined as Democracy — concentration of power in the hands of the few. There may be examples of many newcomers. *Pang- decoration lang sila* (They are only decorations). Look at who wields true power. It's the same few families."

There are many angry young

men and women like my young friend. What we must all realize is that there is a new world awaiting us beyond this century. It will be dynamic and revolutionary. The future will definitely be different from what we have now. New ideas will be born, new ways of thinking and doing things will bring us where we've never been. If we want to be relevant to the coming change, there are many changes we should now make. We should not wait for the social volcano to explode.

Dreams are worthless,

though, without the urgent action to get them done.

I would like to end with an excerpt from Thomas Gray's "Elegy Written in a Country Churchyard" where he spoke of lost opportunities and unfulfilled potentials.

Full many a gem of purest ray serene
The dark unfathomed caves of ocean bear;
Full many a flower is born to blush unseen,
And waste its sweetness on the desert air.

Chapter Two

Solid Corporation

A MISSION BEYOND BUSINESS

For me, there's a mission
beyond business:

To believe, trust, and show faith in our people.

To prove erroneous the oftentimes wrongly accepted belief that business in the Philippines can succeed only through political patronage, bribery of officials to get concessions or franchises, or kowtowing to the powers that be.

I believe in my mission; therefore, I'd like to prove that you can succeed in business too by:

Demanding integrity from yourself and others.

Investing in the goodness and talent of our people.

Being respectful to government officials without having to be subservient or getting something that you will enjoy as an advantage over others.

Distancing yourself from the intrigues, demands, and temptations of politics and politicians.

Believing in a level playing field of doing business even though others do not (they may mouth it but deeds prove them otherwise).

Not burdening any government financial institution with concessionary loans.

Fighting always for the Filipino honor and dignity even in the face of courting displeasure and possibly some punishment from those displeased (both local and foreign).

This kind of business behavior may sound alien in our business society, but with God and total belief in His goodness and justice, I tell you it can be done. The Solid Corporation's story is living proof of this proposition.

Let me tell you our story.

I was still looking for a name

when we were about to incorporate. That day, I went to the bank, The Consolidated Bank and Trust Corporation. The bank president, Willie Tecson, is an old friend of mine. I told him I wanted to open an account for a new company but I could not find a good name.

He said, "Don't look far. Name it Solid. Because our name is very long and nobody remembers us by that name. Our short name is Solid."

So I decided to call my company "Solid Industries, Inc." and we formally registered it on May 5, 1965.

I asked for an amendment some years later to "Solid Corporation" to improve name recall. The funny thing, though, is that people now relate everything "Solid" to me and not to Solid Bank. People even ask me if I own Solid Bank . . .

But Solid's roots

go back much earlier. A decade before Solid Industries, there was already AA Commercial, a small single proprietorship under my name. Its business lines were import and wholesale distribution.

Later, we incorporated AA Commercial. My husband and I worked together to enlarge the business into other activities. We became the exclusive distributors of Asahi glass, Mitsubishi Chemical's synthetic resins (*Yukalon* and *Novatec* brands) which we introduced to the Philippine market in 1959, Otto Meyer's (Germany) *Petromax* brand pressure lanterns, and various canned goods. At this early period, we were already importing and selling Sony transistor radios.

Another company, State Glass, owned by the Chua family and managed by my husband Joseph since 1947, was the biggest importer of Asahi glass (flat sheet, figured, and tinted glass).

The Petromax

pressure lantern business was later transferred to Solid Corporation from AA Commercial for more added value, that is, instead of just importing the product, we would assemble it locally.

We imported Petromax kit parts from Germany. We hired added personnel and set up an assembly line with proper jigs, tools, and some local parts. Solid Corp. then marketed the Petromax pressure lanterns throughout the country via a dealer network. Most of these were sold in the countryside as this product was indispensable to the livelihood of all fishermen and farmers. Furthermore, there was a great absence of electricity in the households and Petromax pressure lanterns did the good job of providing light at night in almost all rural homes.

However, when Otto Meyer decided to put up a Petromax factory in Indonesia, we discontinued it because it was no longer economically viable. Our duties and taxes were too high and imported finished goods eroded our assembled efficacy. Nonetheless, our Petromax assembly episode was a heartwarming experience while it lasted.

The Petromax pressure lantern marketing effort was so successful in the Philippines that people equated pressure lanterns with Petromax, just like Colgate is equated with toothpaste. It was through our efforts that Petromax became a household word.

Many years later, this Petromax business went under because Hong Kong started producing cheaper brands under brand names like Butterfly and Solar which they sold to the Philippines at very much lower prices than Petromax, a premium brand. The price differential was too great for us to surmount. Hong Kong is just next door and completely built-up pressure lanterns at very much reduced prices were great odds for us to overcome. We had to open letters of credit (LCs) all the way to Germany, assemble the product, procure packaging materials locally (at high prices) and give to our dealers 60 to 90 days credit, plus we had to invest substantial funds in promotions and advertising.

On the other hand, the low-cost pressure lanterns from Hong Kong came in complete and rode for free on the goodwill, product awareness and acceptance we had built up through the years. These proved to be tremendous built-in advantages for their products.

This was an example of how one good assembly activity can be adversely affected by parallel imports with less commitments.

Fortunately, we were already assembling Sony TV sets

when the end came for the Petromax business; this enabled us to absorb all the workers in the Petromax line to the electronics line. This way, we avoided the displacement of a good workforce which could have created another social problem.

I would like to recall

an incident here. On August 2, 1968, a huge building in Manila called the "Ruby Tower" collapsed because of a massive intensity 7 earthquake that struck the city. People got trapped inside the building. Rescue work could be done only during the day because there was no electricity at night.

When I heard that the Ruby Tower collapsed and people were trapped inside, I gave instructions to have the Petromax lanterns prepared, filled with gas, tested and ready for use and brought to the collapsed tower. I donated 50 units of Petromax lanterns for the excavation and rescue of those people. It took weeks for the buried bodies to be excavated. Many were buried alive. To recall, there was this remarkable story of a young girl named Suzie who was brought out of the ruins alive after more than 10 days without food and water. She ate all her clothes and she was rescued practically naked.

I would like to believe that for the many saved, my Petromax pressure lanterns played a role in their faster rescue. Later, I was to learn that the Petromax pressure lanterns I donated were used by the fire department for their other activities.

We are all shaped,

for better or for worse, by the political, economic, and cultural environment we find ourselves in. Indeed, the key to understanding our present and future is by understanding our past.

Let me recall the important historical forces that shaped us.

The political environment

during our early years was sizzling hot. Nineteen-sixty-five was right smack in the middle of the turbulent sixties, the time when Filipinos were giddily moving from one election fever to another.

For some mysterious reason, Filipinos seem to be the most election-conscious people in the world. While developed nations have problems generating enough interest and participation from their voters, the opposite is true for Filipinos.

Even the birds

and the dead cast their votes, runs a common joke. Another joke is that there are more votes cast than the number of voters in some areas. But the funniest thing, though, is that often, these are not jokes.

The nation's political fever was in full heat during Solid Corporation's early days.

The year 1960 was the prelude to the 1961 election year. The administration of President Carlos Garcia was about to end, with President Diosdado Macapagal coming into power by 1961.

The next election fever gripped the nation in 1964.

At that time there were only two political parties — Nationalista and Liberal.

The Nationalista Party, in another act of political expediency, decided in 1964 to bring in Ferdinand Marcos, a staunch Liberal partyman, as their official candidate for the Presidency.

For the Nationalistas, having a Liberal partyman as candidate for President was supposed to be a clever strategic and tactical approach to prevent what they felt would be rampant cheating by the then incumbent Liberal Party.

Marcos won the presidency in 1965. He got re-elected in 1969. Barred by the constitution from having a third term, he declared Martial Law on September 21, 1972.

Marcos' rule lasted for over two decades and effected the demise of all political parties. Only the party of Ferdinand Edralin Marcos survived. This was the *Kilusang Bagong Lipunan* ("New Society Movement"), craftily hidden at first as a popular grassroots movement.

The assassination

of Marcos' arch-rival, former Senator Benigno "Ninoy" Aquino, on August 21, 1983, galvanized even the once-timid middle and upper classes to join the popular opposition to Marcos.

This led to the 1986 "Snap Election" between Marcos and Corazon "Cory" Aquino, Ninoy's widow. Predictably, the Marcos-controlled parliament declared him winner of the 1986 snap polls.

The defeated candidate, Cory Aquino, protested and hit the campaign trail for a boycott of businesses identified to be allies and cronies of Marcos. Among such business establishments were the Manila Bulletin, Rustan's, San Miguel Corporation, and several others.

Marcos would have been in power until 1992 but a military coup headed by his Defense Secretary, Juan Ponce Enrile, and Armed Forces Chief of Staff, General Fidel V. Ramos, on February 21 to 25, 1986, ended his rule abruptly.

He was removed from Malacañang and flown to Hawaii by U.S. military plane.

On February 26, 1986, Mrs. Corazon Cojuangco-Aquino was declared the new President; Salvador Laurel as Vice-President.

President Aquino immediately declared

a revolutionary government and made herself a revolutionary head-of-state, with all powers of the executive, legislative, and judicial offices vested in her person.

The Supreme Court was abolished. All the Supreme Court justices were deemed out of office. She appointed her own set of justices.

The Presidential Commission on Good Government (PCGG) was created under Senator Jovito Salonga to run after all the ill-gotten wealth of the Marcoses and their cronies who were deemed to have plundered the nation.

Fifty men and women appointed by Mrs. Aquino drafted a new Constitution which was immediately ratified by the people in a plebiscite. Elections were called for the other elective positions. This was democracy installed in accordance with the 1987 Constitution.

It was in this interesting, exciting, unique, and difficult business environment that Solid struggled to survive and with God's help, managed to prosper.

Half a century has passed

since the Americans turned over its colonial rule to the Filipinos on July 4, 1946. The preoccupation of the Filipino for politics has not waned. It has intensified.

For a country with less than 70 million people, we have a bloated government structure of both elective and appointive positions resulting in inefficiencies and ineffectiveness in addressing the basic needs of the people.

Even in the cities, everything is a problem: roads, bridges, power, water, telephones, housing, transportation, hospitals, medical care, education are either not available, inadequate, or expensive. In the rural areas, the situation is even worse.

Politics saps

the nation's wealth. The ugly head of corruption continues to plague the Filipino. The lure of politics and its perceived glory, honor, security, power, perks, and pelf have a magnetic challenge to many desiring a better life, whether materially or socially. Yet paradoxically, the pay in all government positions is low and below that of the private sector. As many wryly observe, not only do you earn in government, you also have a salary.

In election season or out, politics is the main topic for the Filipino. They forget everything else, including the economy. Right after elections, losers start preparing for the next elections. Winners do the same.

Political backing

is often a prerequisite for entry into government service. Choice positions are given to those who contribute to the political victory of the candidates. Newly elected or appointed officials hire their new personnel and change policies and rules, thus making the bureaucracy more chaotic and re-inventing the wheel on whatever programs/projects were previously made.

Loyalty and devotion to work become personal as the new appointee is indebted to his "boss." He owes his job to him. This is multiplied all over the political pyramid. A network of political proteges is created. This practice weakens the moral fiber of the country and undermines its economic development on a macro scale.

Oftentimes, decisions and actions are personally and politically colored. Political dynasties practically put the nation in the hands of a few families.

Functions and responsibilities overlap

for political reasons. Somehow, we seem to have lost sight of fundamental democratic principles and concepts such as separation of powers to ensure proper checks and balances, as well as effective and efficient governance.

We seem to have forgotten the basics: the legislative branch should legislate, the executive should execute, the judiciary should judge — no more, no less.

Instead of concentrating on purely legislative work, most legislators get involved in sponsoring executive projects such as roads, bridges, schools, hospitals, basketball courts, and similar highly visible "impact projects."

They have legislated for themselves "countrywide development funds" (CDFs) and "congressional initiative allocations" (CIAs), which they can allocate to the executive projects of their choice. However, Philippine mass media often describe the CDFs and CIAs as mere "pork barrel." And recently, the public was treated to the rather unsavory sight of legislators quarreling over who got the bigger pork slices.

This has led to a growing public clamor for legislators to give up their CDFs and CIAs and to concentrate on legislative work instead.

Certain legislators also engage in "investigations in aid of legislation" on virtually every current issue that hogs the headlines. In the process, they virtually become police investigators and judges, all rolled into one. Usually, these investigations do not result in any legislation; instead, they become trials by publicity.

Even if the person on "trial" is later found innocent, the damage to the person's reputation is usually irreparable.

It should be pointed out that it is not only the

individual who is affected but also his/her entire family. For example, the children of the accused often become the butt of jokes in school.

Considering how sacred a reputation is to a person's dignity, such trials by publicity should be stopped.

On the other hand, there are also quite a number of instances when we see the executive branch encroaching on congressional turf, like when the former maneuvers to neutralize all political opposition in Congress, in effect making the latter a homogeneous body that approves, on an almost automatic basis, the "pet bills" of the Executive. This has led to situations wherein Congress finds itself depicted in mass media as the Executive's rubber stamp.

I remember a time

when this was not the case. In the pre-war days, that is, before World War II, and even up to the early sixties, the Philippine Congress concentrated on purely legislative work. The separation of functions and powers was strictly observed.

So what happened? What caused this growing lack of legislative focus?

I think this phenomenon can be traced back to the imposition of Martial Law by former President Ferdinand Marcos. By concentrating all executive, legislative, and judicial powers in his person for almost a decade, Marcos gradually erased the nation's democratic institutions not only legally but also in the hearts and minds of most Filipinos, especially among the younger generation.

As a result, many of today's political leaders have not internalized the true meaning of democracy, of separation of powers. What should have been a historical aberration became convenient practice.

Thus, the constitutional mandate for the separation of powers among the legislative, executive, and judicial branches of government often becomes a farce. A rule observed or violated at the convenience of the current power wielders.

On the lighter side,

I remember a Taiwanese minister's reply when he was asked the "secret" of Taiwan's economic success. He said that Taiwan has very few lawyers, and perhaps this explains why things get done much more quickly in Taiwan. Later, a senior minister from Singapore gave the same explanation for Singapore's rapid growth. They also have very few lawyers in Singapore.

In the Philippines, virtually every family counts one or more lawyers in its clan. With so many lawyers, there's not enough legal work to be done and so, many lawyers end up becoming "ambulance-chasers," that is, people who prey on the misfortunes of others, trying to exacerbate even small conflicts so legal work can be done. By the way, most Filipino politicians — including some of the nation's presidents — are lawyers.

I would be the last to denigrate the legal profession since I'm a lawyer myself. But we should all be brave enough to face even painful truths about ourselves.

We should go back to basics.

Often, legislators justify their sponsorship of infrastructure impact projects as the only way to survive in the Philippine political culture. They say that most Filipinos do not understand what legislative work means. If they don't have billboards proclaiming their sponsorship of this road and that bridge, the voters would not re-elect them.

But if nothing is done, this situation will become an endless cycle resulting in the breakdown of our democratic institutions. The cycle has to stop somewhere, and I think the responsibility for doing so primarily rests on the shoulders of the nation's political leaders.

They should make examples of themselves on how separation of powers can be truly practiced. Of course, this should be complemented by intensive programs to educate the Filipino electorate.

The economic environment

during the sixties was quite healthy. It may sound unbelievable now but the Philippines then was considered next to Japan — in terms of economic growth in our region in Asia, which meant that other Asian economies were even farther behind.

To my mind, the key factors behind our No. 2 position included, among others, substantial post-war American aid, Japanese military reparations, plus the high educational base of our people. The latter is explained by the top priority Filipinos give to education; a farmer would sell his last carabao to send his children to school.

There were such high hopes for our economy to march to prosperity with the Filipino people finally enjoying an enhanced quality of life. Unfortunately, because of political and economic mismanagement, other Asian economies soon overtook the Philippines.

Until today, the dream of a prosperous, equitable, and just Philippine society remains a dream. But we have not lost hope and we are working very hard to make that dream come true.

What greatly strengthens my hopes

are the many positive signs I see which can only mean

better times ahead for the Filipino entrepreneur, in particular, and for the whole country, in general.

This better of times, coming on the heels of one of the nation's most traumatic political episodes and a debilitating power crisis, is a triumph of the Filipino spirit. The Filipino's resiliency, endurance, and optimism have always been his source of greatest hope; the hope that tomorrow will be better. Mere hopes and dreams, as we all know, are never enough. There has to be vision and leadership. The country is blessed with leaders who are capable of great vision, courage, and capacity for hard work. That they were there at a crucial moment in history bodes well for the destiny of this great nation.

President Fidel V. Ramos

is showing admirable leadership. Any contemporary businessman, whether President Ramos' friend or foe, cannot but take notice of the economic reforms he has initiated. As the chief architect of these reforms, the President showed extraordinary swiftness and courage in liberalizing and breaking up the monopolies that used to have a stranglehold on certain industries.

Major changes are being felt in the banking, telecommunications, steel, and power sectors. Companies in these sectors now thrive in an atmosphere of freer competition and are encouraged by the challenges of improving efficiency and providing total quality, market-oriented products and services. The magnitude of President Ramos' leadership and vision is even more remarkable if we consider that many of these were unacted upon by his predecessors.

Credit the President too

for leading and inspiring not a few good men and women

to share his visions and work towards common national objectives. These men and women are inspirations to all of us who are also trying to contribute our best efforts to the daunting task of nation building.

There is Secretary Rizalino S. Navarro of the Department of Trade and Industry (DTI) whose leadership has significantly boosted the country's credibility as a major investment and trading center, and has eased the country's entry into the mainstream of the world's economies. Mr. Navarro's work ethic, illumined judgment, and professionalism have rubbed off on the entire department. I never had as much pleasure and satisfaction dealing with this all-potent government body as I have now.

Among DTI's exemplary executives working with Secretary Navarro are:

Undersecretary Cesar Bautista, in charge of international trade. He is directly responsible for the unparalleled upsurge the country is now enjoying in doing business with the world's major economies.

Undersecretary Melito Salazar, Managing Head of the Board of Investments (BOI), is another fine example who has shown genuine concern for the needs of entrepreneurs and investors.

Governor Ofelia V. Bulaong, also of the BOI, is another deserving mention. She shares the concept of public service being upheld by Undersecretary Bautista and Undersecretary Salazar. These DTI executives exemplify the model public servants entrepreneurs always find satisfaction dealing with. I am in awe of their quick, decisive, and reasoned responses to matters brought to their attention.

Secretary Roberto de Ocampo of the Department of Finance is untiring in his efforts to implement the much needed economic reforms in support of the President's policies. The tax reform package, for instance, is a bold measure to bring down tariffs. I welcome with great satisfaction the apparent shift in the Bureau of Customs' orientation from one of revenue generation to the provision of promotions/services for exporters and importers. The business sector is supportive of this major shift as well as the policies of Secretary de Ocampo.

Former Bureau of Internal Revenue (BIR) Commissioner Jose Ong is equally noteworthy. Under his term, government revenue collections reached record levels.

Bureau of Customs (BOC) Commissioner Guillermo Parayno should be commended for the BOC's computerization program and the reactivation of the Customs-Industry Consultative Council (CICC) founded by former Customs Commissioner Salvador M. Mison.

When I speak of the BOC, I cannot help but mention the name of former Commissioner Mison who, to my mind, offered public service with exemplary professional work ethic, where justice, fair play, and commitment to public service were always at the forefront.

The telecommunications sector is at the forefront of reforms and major changes, thanks in no small measure to the proactivism and boldness of leaders like Secretary Amado Luis S. Lagdameo and Undersecretary Josefina Lichauco, both of the Department of Transportation and Communications, and Mr. Simeon Kintanar of the National Telecommunication Commission. They have the formidable task of bringing the country's telecommunications capability to world class standards in and with the most limited time and resources. Yet the urgency with which this hardy group is plunging into this seemingly mission impossible is simply contagious.

The dynamism of Governor Gabriel Singson of the *Bangko Sentral ng Pilipinas* (Central Bank of the Philippines) is sweeping through the banking sector. Governor Singson oversaw the design and implementation of the structures and policies governing the liberalized Philippine financial system. We are feeling the effects now of better service by banks, lower interest and inflation rates, and a relatively stable peso. It is not exaggeration if bankers, exporters and importers consider Governor Singson a visionary.

Secretary Gregorio R. Vigilar of the Department of Public Works and Highways continues to inspire with his tireless dedication to accelerate infrastructure development. His reputation for honesty has restored much of the credibility to, and self-respect in, a department previously tainted with past scandals and questionable dealings.

I also had occasions to observe the dedication and competence of government executives, some of whom have rejoined private industry. Executives and managers like Messrs. Victor Lim and Antonio Henson, formerly of the Clark Development Authority; present administrators Richard Gordon of Subic Bay Development Authority and General Romeo David of Clark Development Authority. These dedicated and extremely capable gentlemen are responsible for the great economic strides the country is taking especially in the area of investments and industrialization in all former U.S. bases in the country.

Let us not forget

the many unsung heroes, too many to mention, in both public and private sectors, who despite low pay and often less-than-ideal working conditions, continue to contribute their labor and expertise towards economic success. There are also the countless entrepreneurs, industrialists, exporters, importers, and service providers who through their efforts and investments are creating thousands of new jobs. Together with government, they are making people empowerment closer to reality.

The electronics consumer industry

was yet to be developed in the sixties. At the forefront were pioneer companies like Ysmael Steel, Radiowealth, Radiola, and the Del Rosario family's Precision Electronics Corporation.

All were Filipino-owned and managed because there was a prohibition at that time for multinationals to get into this kind of industry. At that time, there was also a restriction in the foreign exchange, which was greatly regulated by the Central Bank.

However, these companies mostly imported the consumer products they were selling and, at best, were making simple assembly. Through this process, the Philippines was able to introduce electronic products to the market. It was a good start.

Sony in the fifties

and early sixties was not the Sony that it is today.

It was just a modest and upcoming radio and black and white television maker in Japan.

In 1959, Sony finally came out with their first color TV — Chromatron. They borrowed the technology from the United States and it was a failure. Sony discontinued the assembly of Chromatron color TV because it fell below their expectations of a good quality color television. Instead, they developed their own Trinitron which was a tremendous success.

I saw the great potential of Sony Although it had a limited product, it had great potential because of the leadership of the Sony group — people who came out with the philosophy that they would go into areas where nobody dared to go. Do intensive research. Open up fields no man would go into. I fell in love with this philosophy and I said to myself, "This company will go far."

So when we established Solid Industries in 1965, we decided to focus our sales on the consumer electronics of Sony. We went into an enthusiastic and dedicated campaign to market whatever Sony products we could get our hands on.

At this time, in the Philippines Sony was many years behind the other established companies making consumer electronic products   under various brand names such as Radiowealth, Zenith, Admiral, General Electric, National, Sharp, Hitachi, Sanyo, Philips, and Toshiba. However, because of the strategy we used in promoting Sony, we made it what it is today — the No. 1 brand in the Philippines for electronic consumer products, especially in color television, VCR, and high-end audio hi-fi components.

"White line" and "brown line"

are basic terms in the electronics industry which may sound strange to laymen.

"White line" refers to household electrical appliances such as refrigerators, stoves and ranges, washing machines, electric fans, rice cookers, toasters, blenders, flat irons, and the like.

"Brown line" covers electronic consumer products like TV, VCRs, cassette recorders, and other audio/video equipment.

Why "white," why "brown," someone once asked me. Well, it seems that the most logical explanation on how these terms came about is that during the early days, most household appliances were painted white (thus "white line"), while TV and stereo sets often came in brown wooden cabinets (thus "brown line").

Since Sony concentrates on the brown line and is not into the white line, Solid also got the exclusive distributorship from National for a broad range of white line products. In fact, we introduced and popularized the first National brand gas stove in the Philippines. This was no small feat, considering that we had to educate Filipino consumers that there was no basis to the widespread misconception that gas stoves were "dangerous" because they could "easily explode." Today, the gas stove is a regular fixture in most Filipino households.

However, by 1970, we dropped all our involvement with the white line products because of our committed focus to promote Sony electronic consumer products.

Even today, many Sony officials

are stymied by the fact that the Philippines, through Solid, is the only country in the world that has an *exclusive* technical licensing agreement with Sony. In all other countries, Sony's local partners have *non-exclusive* status.

But we have proven how justly deserving we are of the trust because despite the Sony brand being the last to enter the electronics consumer market (in the days of quantitative restriction policy of the government), we have made the image and name Sony unsurpassed in the Philippines. To own and use a Sony is a joy and a pride.

Actually, we started selling Sony transistor radios in the early sixties. We purchased the radios and sold them mainly in Manila. This humble beginning was accelerated in the next decade, thus building a good foundation and earning Sony's trust to give us an exclusive manufacturing licensing agreement in 1971.

The rest, as they say, is history.

The first big thorn

we endured was the accreditation process with the Board Of Investments (BOI) which proceeded at a turtle's speed. Believe it or not, it took us three years to get accredited as a local TV manufacturer.

In 1971, as part of its import-substitution thrust, government instituted the Electronics Local Content Program (ELCP).

The program called for "added value." There must be local content. Either you do certain things locally or purchase them locally.

In support of the ELCP, and in consultation with the BOI, the Bureau of Internal Revenue (BIR) came up with Revenue Memorandum No. 1-71 which mandated certain parts to be sourced locally. "Completely built-up" (CBU) television sets were prohibited from importation. It also gave long-existing companies already accredited by the BOI the privilege of paying only seven per cent (7%) sales tax on the sale of finished products — while those without accreditation had to pay 40% sales tax. This policy was meant to protect local manufacturers so they could improve their production process and compete strongly in the world market.

This program favored

long-existing companies because the parts that were supposed to be sourced locally under the new rules were already conceded to them. In effect, they were allowed to continue importing those parts.

But for newcomers like Solid, the law was strictly enforced.

Right away, you could see that there was discrimination and bias. It was imperative that I be accredited. An application was made. I felt that this kind of a rule gave an outright advantage to those companies who were automatically accredited, simply by their being in prior existence. Newcomers like me had to go through the bureaucratic process of application, inspection of our plant by a team from BOI-BIR and representatives of the accredited companies, and endorsement by the BOI-BIR team before we could get BOI approval.

If you want to kill competition,
you couldn't have thought of a better process. To think that this program was conceived and implemented by "technocrats" (a term coined to refer to those people in government who are supposed to have outstanding expertise and intelligence).

When I first applied for the accreditation with the BOI, it was outrightly denied. Not by the Board, because it had not yet reached the Board. It was denied by two members of the Evaluation Group who sent out the denial.

As far as I can remember, there was an absolutely bureaucratic and biased attitude against me by those two people who suddenly found power in their position and really made it difficult for an unknown applicant to get through.

I suffered terribly during those months because I couldn't compete freely, obviously because of the 40% sales tax. I felt that the whole thing was unfair and unjust, not only to me but to all who were similarly situated. It so happened that I was the only one applying at that time (all the other major brands had already been accredited).

Because of my strong passion and vision that Sony would become a great name in the electronics industry, that the Filipino people should not be denied a product of very high quality, I determined that I would not let this first denial derail me. It strengthened my resolve to do more so I wrote a reconsideration letter.

Without even bothering

to read my letter of reconsideration, the same persons threw it out and said that they were not allowed to entertain reconsiderations. The rule calls for a new application. Once an application is denied, you cannot ask for a reconsideration. You must reapply.

I found this procedure ridiculous. Why should I reapply when every basis of my application remains the same? What was called for was simply a reconsideration.

At this juncture,

a certain official advised me to engage the services of a law firm then known to be well-connected with the powers that be (Martial Law was already instituted on September 21, 1972). I was made to understand that if anybody could help me, it was "The Law Firm" of the day.

I took the advice and with the recommendation of this government official, engaged the services of The Firm, hoping that my application could be acted upon more expeditiously. I gave all the documentation and the pertinent data required by the BOI.

Six months passed and I did not hear

any news from The Firm. I inquired repeatedly and each time I was told that they were still studying my papers.

One of the lawyers, however, told me that I had somehow antagonized some personnel in the BOI because of my stubborn refusal to file a new application and my insistence on my letter of reconsideration instead. Hence, they had not filed my papers yet.

I was astounded by this comment. I thought it silly how the procedural aspect of the case can cause such a heavy weight for the firm to study my application lengthily. However, I was willing to wait some more. I had no other recourse. I did not have a *padrino* (godfather) to help me. This matter of having *padrinos* is a pervasive and continuing problem. For me, it is a practice which violates the principle of fair play.

Even today I hear so many small and medium enterprises (SMEs) complain about the *padrino* system. As early as the seventies, the same problem existed.

Who says I am aggressive? It's far from the truth. I swallow personal pride and practice humility most of the time. It's only when one is pushed against the wall and there's no other way to go but to bounce back that I shed off my humble garb and fight and seek for justice.

It's cowardly to yield when I feel I am in the right. But in every struggle, every fight for a cause, I practice utmost decorum and respect for the rights of others. I have never been abrasive. I seek for a peaceful resolution as much as possible. But I never sacrifice a fundamental principle or value in the process.

Many more months were to pass

before I finally went to The Firm and requested for the return of all my papers.

I decided to appeal my case directly to the chairman of the BOI. I sought an audience with him and explained my case.

In my meeting with the chairman, I insisted that the BOI act on my case on its merits and not simply deny the request for reconsideration on a question of procedure.

Without evaluating the merits of my application, it was denied on the ground that the analyst was unable to examine our books. I countered that when the analyst went to our factory, it was "on strike" and we could not get inside to get the books for examination. Besides, how could he pass judgment on the factory operations when the same was closed due to a labor problem?

But now that the strike had been settled, and the factory back in operation, he was welcome to visit the plant and go over the books.

With this explanation, the chairman allowed the reconsideration to be accepted.

You would think this solved

the matter. No way. The officers who denied the application at first instance were out to get me. They sat on it. This was during the oppressive days of martial rule and all we could do was wait and wait. It was only in 1975 that Solid Corporation got its accreditation.

Can you imagine

how a simple accreditation could take that long? It is because the system is a bureaucratic one which relies more on procedural features rather than on substantive factors.

Also, personal prejudices could have caused the long delay. It was not until the officials who first denied it left the BOI that my application was acted upon. All those past years, not only was I not able to compete, but worse, I suffered losses. I had a hard time just trying to survive.

I find it strange that in other ASEAN countries,

they help and and promote local entrepreneurs proactively. No one takes you for granted. In my country, I may be wrong but because of what I went through at that point in my life, it is my feeling that oftentimes, multinationals have an advantage over local applicants.

It is especially difficult if you are small, unknown, and without any political connection, and when you are just starting out.

I admire the multinationals who usually "unite" and address their problems with support from their respective associations. When there's unity, there's strength. How well they know this principle and practice it fully!

The second thorn

was the seemingly simple matter of sourcing TV tuners that, thanks to government technocrats, became a most convoluted, life-and-death issue for Solid.

After we obtained our accreditation in 1975 as a domestic manufacturer, the BOI included in its Electronic Local Content Program (ELCP) the local sourcing of TV tuners.

The BOI assumed that the existing manufacturers who were accredited before 1975 were already manufacturing their own tuners or buying them locally without really finding out whether there already were domestic manufacturers of TV tuners.

This requirement again prevented us from strongly competing with the more established TV brands since our TV production volume was unnecessarily limited by this new restriction.

A tuner

is a vital component of a TV set since it captures the

radio signals from the TV stations and allows channel selection.

It was therefore necessary that we had to have adequate supply of tuners so that we could produce the volume we knew we could sell. But Solid, having been accredited only in 1975, could not import its TV tuners or tuner parts. Neither could we source any locally because there was none locally available.

We went from one company to another asking them to sell us TV tuners. None would. None could. Besides, Sony was already using miniaturized TV tuners which the other TV manufacturers were not capable of producing as they were using the bigger type tuners.

Our competitors had no problem with this new BOI requirement since they were accredited before 1975 and were therefore allowed to import TV tuner parts. But in fact, they only imported very few tuner parts which they assembled from screwdriver-type operations. Most of their TV tuner importations were completely built units needing no further assembly work in the Philippines; worse, they misdeclared the tuners, passing them off as radio parts which had lower tariff rates than TV tuners.

Thus, a no-win situation
confronted Solid. A very cruel situation created by technocrats supposedly to benefit the Filipino. It was more than enough to discourage anyone with less gumption and determination.

So while Solid was already accredited as a domestic producer, we still had to request BOI approval each time we needed TV tuners. But the approval would come in trickles like 500 pieces each time. For the next three years, we floundered. Our sales were limited. Our factory could not expand. We remained pegged down to small volumes. There was not enough work for our employees. Our situation gave great advantage to our competitors.

Just to keep our people working, we got Sony's approval to assemble/manufacture black-and-white television for export to Central America at great sacrifice and loss to us. Our volume was not big enough to offset expenditures. The export selling price was barely enough to meet the cost of parts purchased (both imported and local), manufacturing costs, and administrative costs. Yet this exercise, difficult as it was, gave us tremendous experience and knowledge on the intricacies of exporting. We certainly made no profits, but we gained a worldful of experience and values.

Towards the end

of this three-year period, I found myself at the crossroads of whether to give up my manufacturing operation of Sony color TVs or to go into TV tuner manufacturing, which was included in the government's investment priority program, so that I could effectively compete in the marketplace.

I realized, however, that the technology for TV tuner manufacturing, especially tuners for Sony televisions, was not easily available and those who had it, like the Japanese, were not too willing to share this with anybody else.

My very strong feeling about the Sony brand made me decide that I must go into TV tuner manufacturing. But how could I acquire the technology, I asked myself. Finally, in 1978, I decided to seek the help of Dr. Susumo Yoshida, manufacturing head of Sony in Japan. I explained to him our difficulty in expanding our color TV production and our strong desire to aggressively market Sony color TV as No. 1 in the Philippines someday. To do this, we needed to solve the problem of sourcing TV tuners.

It was Dr. Yoshida who made the arrangements so we could be introduced to the biggest tuner maker of Japan, Murata, which was also supplying tuners to almost all TV makers in Japan, including Sony. With the help of Sony Corporation, Murata agreed to supply us with their technology on TV tuner manufacturing.

Thus armed

with Murata's technology, I went back to the BOI and signified my intention to invest in TV tuner manufacturing on a pioneer status.

Then Deputy Trade and Industry Minister Edgardo Tordesillas who was also concurrent managing head of the BOI required us to submit our feasibility study within 60 days. He listened to my explanation that the current price of a tuner was about P145.00 per piece and if I was allowed to manufacture it, I could make it at much less and sell it locally at not more than P100.00 per piece. This would help to reduce the cost of TV sets and benefit the consumers.

Subsequently, I received a call from Deputy Minister Tordesillas who informed me that he had arranged a meeting between me and the Concepcions (owners of Concepcion Industries) who owned Electro Components, Inc. (ECI), a company already registered with the BOI and applying for TV tuner manufacturing.

Realizing that it was the fastest way for me to go into TV tuner manufacturing, I met with the Concepcions and we eventually agreed to go on a joint venture in ECI. The idea was to utilize Murata technology to make tuners for the local TV manufacturers, including Solid.

At that time, the landed cost of a tuner was about P130.00 to P140.00 per piece and the selling price was

P145.00 to P150.00 per piece. We were buying our tuners at that price. With the Murata technology, competent sourcing of parts and raw materials, and the excellent skills of the Filipinos, we computed that ECI could sell the tuners at not more than P100.00 each and still make good profits. With this situation, we hoped that at last we could bring some sanity to the tuner problem.

Logic would dictate

that if you were a local TV manufacturer, you would be glad that you could locally source tuners at a much lower cost than if you import or "make" them in-house. And the tuners were readily available at 30 to 60 days credit term. If this same opportunity was presented to me in the past seven years, during the entire time that I was greatly disadvantaged having been denied the right to import tuners or buy them from my competitors, I would have shouted in great exultation!

But now that my company made tuners locally, none of the existing local TV manufacturers bothered to buy from us despite all the seemingly good benefits. They preferred to source from their mother companies abroad and practically boycotted and ignored the tuner manufacturing facility of ECI. What happened was "Japan, Inc." at work. It is what has made Japan a strong and developed nation.

Consequently, ECI only had one customer — Solid Corporation. ECI could not go into mass production. Our dream of hiring many hundreds of employees ended up in only 100 workers. There was something wrong with the implementation of government policy. Basic principles of logic were violated. There was just no rhyme or reason, but then that was reality: an unsavory situation.

Many years later, I brought the situation to the attention

of a senior BOI official who called for a meeting of all the BOI registered local TV manufacturers. In that meeting, the division chief handling the electronics sector brought files of import documents with him showing the details of importations made by the TV manufacturers. He reported to the senior BOI official that the import documents of these companies showed no importations of TV tuners, whether as parts or as complete units. Since it was not possible to make TV sets without tuners, the tuners must have been brought in under different description or commodity classification.

Confronted with the documents,

the president of one local TV manufacturer said that as president of his company, he was not involved in the details of operations or importation, but if the records showed what the BOI reported, then the facts must be so.

The executive of another manufacturer remarked that the companies must have the flexibility to cut cost, as a business decision, even if it meant that tuners are classified as radio parts in their importations. To this last remark, the senior BOI official said that if companies want to misclassify their importations, they could do so provided they stay out of the BOI program, meaning that they would be subject to 40% sales tax instead of just 7%.

The meeting was adjourned with promises from the other TV manufacturers to abide by the rules. They also made a verbal request that they be condoned for the misclassification they did in past importations to avoid paying the right tariff.

In the end, nothing productive came out of it. ECI still was left with one customer — us. Only at a much later period did some of the TV makers order tuners from ECI. But the quantity was quite small and by then, it was too late.

The Concepcions were not happy with how the tuner business was turning out. They eventually sold their shares to us. They left ECI to fight the injustice. It took another three years before we appealed to the BOI to give some rationality to the tuner problem. But by then, Solid was already able to produce color TV at the quantity the market needed. And despite having only Solid as its lone customer, ECI has managed to keep its workforce up to the present.

The third thorn

was the Cathode Ray Tube (CRT) problem. (CRT is the picture tube in a TV set.)

Again, the black-and-white CRT was supposed to be procured locally. But there was no CRT factory that could produce the quantity required by the growing industry at competitive pricing. There were three CRT makers then but they were producing mostly for their own needs. One of them was a possible source for us but it was unable to produce the volume that we needed at the delivery time agreed upon. Since we were exporting black-and-white TV sets, we needed a greater quantity of 12-inch picture tubes, and they did not have the capability to do it.

We solved this by going into black-and-white CRT manufacturing. We were then able to export black-and-white television sets because of the CRT tubes that our own factory produced.

The fourth thorn

was the "NIVICO problem."

Sometime during the Martial Law period, certain influential businessmen close to President Marcos thought of a way to undersell legitimate local TV manufacturers by importing black-and-white TV duty and tax-free.

The official justification for this scheme was that people in the countryside, especially the poor, needed to have access to low-cost black-and-white TV so that mass information and education programs could reach them.

To cloak his cronies with legitimacy, Marcos issued an executive order which authorized a certain company to bring in television duty and tax free for the purpose of helping the poor in the provinces.

The program as defined under the executive order called for the company to manufacture the TV sets locally. But it turned out to be a "screwdriver operation" because the company brought in the TV sets almost complete and, with a screwdriver, put them together and sold them. Worse, these TV sets were all brought to the urban areas and competed with local manufacturers who had to comply with the component and foreign exchange parts limitation.

The TV sets were supplied by a Japanese company and sold under the brand name NIVICO.

Thus, with a stroke of a pen, the growth of the TV industry was crushed. Who can compete against such odds?

Four counts of unfairness

surfaced against the NIVICO "local manufacturer": entry under duty and tax free status; no manufacturing plant needed; no local parts required; sold mostly in Metro Manila and other urban areas.

The executive order was meant to give undue advantage to this company and even Mrs. Alita Martel, an officer of the Central Bank, reported huge revenue losses to the government amounting to hundreds of millions of pesos.

It wasn't only the government revenues that were lost. Worse, Filipinos were denied employment and technology because we favored foreign employment to be subsidized.

As a result, several black-and-white TV manufacturers closed shop. They went bankrupt, not because they were incompetent manufacturers, but because unfair competition drove them out of the market.

The fifth thorn
was the foreign exchange problem.

After the oil debacle brought the peso to its knees, oil prices escalated and commodity prices soared erratically. Consequently, there was an absence of new investments. Factories were unable to operate normally. Expansion was out of the question due to credit crunch, dollar scarcity, and worst of all, the loss of our credibility as a nation to manage our economy.

We helplessly fell under the supervision of the IMF. We had to meekly follow their bitter antidote, like automatically apportioning a huge portion of our nation's revenues, 50% as a starter, to pay for our external debts; increasing oil prices to raise revenues; requiring the private sector to generate foreign exchange for their imports through their own export proceeds.

Thus was born the "Binondo Central Bank," an unofficial but well-organized vehicle used by then Trade Minister Roberto Ongpin to purchase dollars through the black market.

It was a critical period that needed critical solutions such as this scheme conceived by the DTI Secretary, otherwise business would have come to an abrupt halt.

Fortunately for the Solid Group,
our companies had been doing exports in both electronics and marine products, specifically black tiger prawns.

So while we used to just turn over to the Central Bank all our export proceeds and apply our foreign exchange requirements through letter of credit for our imports, we now found ourselves with more than enough foreign exchange for our own use; we could even afford to assign them to other importers/exporters.

The scarcity of dollars was a problem to the other companies who were not involved in exports. They had to cut down their operations, lay off workers, scale down benefits and wages, and many simply closed their companies/operations altogether.

The sixth thorn
was the problem of strikes.

Labor is always an uncertainty in any business, particularly in factory operations. The best and highest paying company is just as much subject to the strike problem as the medium enterprise like mine where the employees number several hundreds.

The first strike we had was in 1969, the second in 1971. Both were quickly resolved in a month or two.

The third took place a decade later. This time it took much more than two months to settle. We shut down the factory. There were no parts available for manufacture.

The demand of the union leaders was very much different from those of its members. The members were clamoring for return to work and it was only the union officers who were adamant.

In a final meeting called by the arbiter, all the workers demanded for a return to work order and were willing to sacrifice their officers. In a spirit of amity, my factory general manager got back the union president under his custody and this was an unexpected turn of event. It was already agreed that the union officers be dismissed; only non-officers could return to work. Why did my factory G.M. request me to allow the union president to return to work under his custody?

Against my better judgment, I acceded readily because it is important to me that I support my G.M. at all times. If he felt he could manage him, who am I to distrust his judgment in his territorial jurisdiction, so to speak. It is his arena. He should know. Peace reigned again. But from then on, every CBA renewal became a very tortuous and tedious exercise.

We have had two more strikes after that (the last one in 1993). Each has been actually a no-win situation for all. Everybody loses. Fortunately, through honest and positive dialogues between management and workers, a much more harmonious and productive working environment has been established since then in all our factories.

As part of our expansion activities, we have also established new companies and factories. We have hired better-educated, younger, and more highly-motivated people. Because of these measures, we now have higher productivity, greater experience, superior quality, and deeper values in the personal lives of all our people.

The seventh thorn

involved two huge floods in the early seventies and nineties when the Tullahan river in Bulacan overflowed. The water was up to five feet high in our factory premises. All the electronic parts in our Sony factory in Valenzuela floated away. There were heavy losses. But we were able to overcome them. Those that we could salvage, we salvaged.

In the first flood, I remember a comical incident. There were some mechanical parts that had to be immediately cleaned and dried, otherwise they would become rusty and unusable. This emergency situation required instant action . . . I immediately borrowed a few hair dryers from my friends and the company also bought additional hair dryers.

Because time was of the essence, we had the employees dry the metal parts. And according to my friends, when they lent their dryers to me, they were very nice hair dryers. By the time I returned them, *nakatungo na* (they were drooping). That was funny. Of course, I had to replace them with brand new ones plus notes of deep appreciation for their help.

I must also commend the alertness of our guards during the flooding. They immediately opened the factory gate when the flood started, thus making the water flow out more quickly. This prevented the water inside the factory premises from rising higher and doing greater damage.

But for every thorn,

there is a greater joy. There have been many beautiful shining moments in the life of our company and people. Let me count the blessings that far outweigh the thorns — character-building blessings — because they are intrinsic to our growth.

The greatest joy

is Achievement.

We cannot measure the tremendous innate satisfaction in finally surmounting seemingly insurmountable problems such as:

Starting a decade behind the others in the industry.

Having scarce logistical and credit support when we needed them most.

Our total lack of political "*padrinos*."

Our poverty of "connections" in government offices.

Our lack of technology as compared to our competitors who were mostly multinationals.

We managed to survive

the difficult start-up years, the uneven playing field, the powers and logistics of the competitors. We were able to resist the temptation to take shortcuts. And today, after three decades, we find ourselves the No.1 electronic consumer durable manufacturer in the Philippine market, besting all multinational companies.

The happiness comes not from dollars and cents or pesos and centavos; it is an inner and exquisite kind of happiness that Filipinos can do well even with all the odds against them.

The joy of proving our self-worth . . .

There was a time in the history of Solid Corporation that we had a Japanese plant overseer.

Since we are manufacturing Sony products with the Sony brand name for the domestic and export markets, it is imperative for Sony to send their representative to check into the quality standards of our company. Thus, for seven years, our people worked under the close supervision of the Japanese expert.

But there was restlessness

in the manufacturing sector. After seven years of intensive training under the Japanese manager, most of the Filipino engineers wanted to show their worth as a very innovative and progressive team without having an expat (the Japanese) breathing down their necks every inch of the way. They wanted the freedom.

This was a very difficult situation. It was but natural

that Sony should have a man here because of the great value of their name, a name they have earned through great achievement and labor.

Knowing how important it was that this man be there to safeguard the interest of Sony, yet at the same time feeling the restlessness of my people, I really had to study carefully whether it was within me to convince Sony to recall their expat home and give us our independence — with the assurance that we will continue to make products equal to what is made in Japan both for domestic and export sales.

But to do this was not an easy task. It meant violating a fundamental policy of any company like Sony that they have full access to all aspects of the manufacturing process.

With deep study and intense prayers to the Lord (more of the latter), I decided to make a trip to Japan to meet the head of Sony's manufacturing wing in Japan, Dr. Susumo Yoshida.

Dr. Yoshida is a living treasure

of Sony, being the founder and the inventor of the Trinitron, a man who has propelled Sony to great heights with his exemplary performance in manufacturing.

For his contributions to the growth of Japanese industry as well as to the growth of the electronics industry around the world, he has received two awards from His Majesty the Emperor of Japan: the Medal of Honor with Purple Ribbon (1973) and the Order of the Sacred Treasure, Gold Rays with Neck Ribbon (1993). He has also been a recipient of numerous awards from various prestigious institutions in Japan.

A senior general manager of Sony once said: "When I face Dr. Yoshida, I keep my eyes down, because he is like a god. He is a genius yet so full of goodness, so kind . . ."

This is the man I went to see. He treated me to a beautiful French dinner at Maxim's in Tokyo. Seeing him across the dinner table, I had no idea at all what I had to say to him, because I had no fully conceived plan of what to say that would be right. We talked of everything under the sun, but I couldn't bring myself to tell him what I wanted.

My objective was to make him understand . . . to allow us to be self-reliant and not to send any Japanese manager to replace the one assigned to us who was scheduled to leave, considering that we already had seven years of their expert tutelage.

Besides, the Filipinos' sense of pride, honor, and dignity in their work was marred by the thought of having an expat looking over their shoulders daily. Though they work very hard, the fact that there is a Japanese manager somehow robs them of the pure joy of achievement, of the ecstasy, the satisfaction of having done everything by themselves. As engineers and creative professionals, they wanted some freedom. They wanted to be trusted. They wanted to show their worth.

Finally, before the meal

was ended, it just came to me, like God putting words into my mouth. It wasn't planned. It just came from me freely, and I said, "Dr. Yoshida, I can't thank you enough for all these seven years that you have nurtured us in the technology of Sony in producing high-quality Sony products. I thank you for the lessons, for the technical expertise, for helping our engineers who go to Japan, and sending us this general manager in our factory. They have been very essential, beneficial, and truly helpful.

"However, I now come to a stage where there is a

strong sense of restlessness and uneasiness in the hearts of my engineers and workforce. Their heart is not fully in the job anymore because they feel that their total worth is not being recognized.

"I know that you have a new engineer who will be coming soon to replace the general manager who is going home; if only I could catch your heart and let you listen to the cry of my people to allow them just a breathing spell; give them a six-month period to show their worth. If it's possible not to send anybody yet. They will live by all your strict standards. They will work and show you that they can do it and it will restore their morale.

"I know that you are helping me a lot, but this is something invisible. It's the value, the worth. And I know that your family comes from a family of barons with nobility in their soul. This is what this is all about. It's not about dollars and cents. It's not about materialism. It's about the restoration of pride, honor, nobility, in the Filipino people who feel that they want this break.

"I don't know if this is possible. I think I may be asking a big thing from you. I assure you, sir, that at the very first inkling that something is wrong, you can send somebody right away. In the meantime, please just give them a breathing spell. If you can only understand . . . I need this for the long haul. Our people will be forever grateful that you trusted us. We need you to believe in us. I have so much faith in my people that I ask you to share this faith with me. Can you do this for me, only for six months? If you could only realize the resounding effect that it will have on your products as well, it will be worth the trust."

He pondered.
He did not make any sound. Just like a Japanese. Slowly,

gently, he nodded his head. But the Japanese nodding does not mean a yes. It means "I have heard you."

So we had dessert. Then I went back to my hotel much relieved that I had poured my heart out. I thought, Oh God, I don't know where I found the words. I don't know how it came out. How could it have been better conveyed? All these thoughts nagged me.

I flew back to Manila, not knowing what the answer would be, because it was a very big thing that I asked for.

There was no reply

for the next two months. But neither did the substitute arrive. The incumbent overseer was still in place, awaiting his replacement. Then came the reply: "We regret to inform you that at this moment we cannot send a replacement because we are short of personnel." Hallelujah!

Everyone was really against my going to Sony for this. They knew it was an impossible mission. Imagine — we were making Sony for export. How could we ask them not to have a representative here? How could that be possible? But the Lord made it possible. God works in mysterious ways. He willed it that Dr. Yoshida would be there at that time. And I believe up to now that only a Dr. Yoshida would understand our predicament. You see, he is from the nobility. He has a very noble character with a deep understanding of human nature.

For his immeasurable support to us in all the stages of our manufacturing operations, we are deeply indebted. Yet, his support to us would still be magnified many times when in 1994 he favored us to manufacture Aiwa color TV for export to Japan, Middle East, Europe and the United States. Aiwa is a subsidiary company of Sony Corporation.

Contributing to countryside development
is another great joy.

Solid has contributed to improving the standard of living through communications via television. Solid introduced many firsts in the Philippine market on electronic products. We introduced the Betamax VCR as early as 1979 and our market was the last market in the world to give up Betamax. Till today, we still sell Betamax. Many exciting products like the walkman, various CD, MD, Karaoke players were made to suit the Filipino taste. We established warehouses, sales branches, and an intensive service network all over the countryside in almost every province, with adequate and efficient personnel to address the services required by all our customers.

Excellent post-sales
customer service is also a source of great happiness and pride for us.

The joy is that we were able to put up 28 Sony service centers all over the country for the past two decades.

Distribution of Sony's products nationwide calls for opening up Solid branches for sales and servicing in all major cities and municipalities. While we have 28 branches now, every year we add two to three more branches.

This phenomenal growth has contributed both to the national and local governments in revenues, job generation, technology and values enhancement among others.

We are the only manufacturer with this kind of sales, service, and warehousing network. Many other companies prefer to subcontract, but we want to ensure quality of parts, quality of work, and we are doing it as a service, as part of our philosophy that every consumer is a satisfied consumer, up to the end of the life of the unit.

In Japan, they keep parts only up to three years, but our service network keeps parts up to seven years (or even longer) because Filipinos normally keep their sets for more than 10 years. They keep on bringing their TV sets back for repair. It is a Filipino culture. It's a culture of thrift, one admirable trait. Unfortunately, if stretched too far, it sometimes becomes a problem to keep parts inventory beyond seven to 10 years.

We had to make wooden cabinets

for television. Later this was supplanted by plastic and now we have the biggest tv/audio plastic cabinet factory in the country.

From 1971 up to the mid-eighties, television and audio sets were fitted with wooden cabinets. We had to subcontract the production of these cabinets to cabinet makers. Since most of these cabinet-makers were found outside the cities, this also became one way of helping in the dispersal of business to the countryside.

Our requirements called for special workmanship on wooden cabinets which necessitated extra-care painting/finishing polish on the cabinets to make them shine like delicate furniture pieces.

Since our subcontractors were not trained to do this kind of workmanship on wooden materials, we helped them upgrade their quality by providing cash advances for them to buy better and special equipment and finishes and had Sony engineers come from Tokyo to give them technology on cabinets fitted for electronic products.

This lasted for many years until the technology on

plastic cabinet was introduced to replace the wooden cabinets which were susceptible to scratches and even termite (*"bok-bok"* in the vernacular) infestation.

With the entry of the plastic cabinet, we had to order our cabinets from the plastic making companies. As our demands grew and the existing companies were unable to meet our requirements, we had to make new plastic plants to address our needs both for domestic and export sales.

Today we have two big plastic injection plants which are fully utilized to meet our present needs. However, as our exports have expanded tremendously, we are beefing up our injection machines to cope with the increased exports. Today, we rank among the biggest plastic makers in the country. We will continue to expand as our market share increases.

Since 1975,

as an accredited manufacturer, I have given my best effort to lift Solid Corporation to be a good and competitive electronic consumer manufacturer. It is very important for me to compete openly under a level playing field and succeed. Besides, as an exclusive manufacturer of Sony in the Philippines, I have to make good. I have to compete against the multinationals who have vast financial resources and a big headstart.

During our early years, I had lots of catching up to do. It meant beefing up the personnel complement, improving our technological capability through more training for our engineers in Sony factories in Tokyo, increasing our local content requirements, adding machineries and equipment, and improving our sales and service network.

How do you do these under martial rule when there's so much political, economic and social uncertainty under a military regime which touts a new social order? How? It wasn't easy. It meant lots of hard work, perseverance, patience, and teamwork.

All kinds of problems

had to be met simultaneously. Aside from the problems earlier mentioned, we had to solve all our production problems which involved parts procurement, quality assurance of parts and finished goods, production flow, inventory, systems and methods plans, management of logistics and personnel, maintenance of supplies, materials, machines, just-in-time deliveries (incoming and outgoing), and so on. There's no end to improvement on quality and process. It's an endless pursuit for excellence.

And finally to marketing challenges. We were competing against entrenched multinationals with vast resources. Not only did we have to catch up to get our market niche, we also had to excel and be No. 1 in sales. This was a tall order indeed!

While our competitors have a wide range of products covering both white and brown lines to attract dealers and consumers, we do not have such diversity of products in Solid. Like Sony, we exclusively handle the brown line of electronic consumer products.

This alone is an added advantage to our competitors. Yet, despite this advantage, we proved our worth by besting them and making Sony the most respected and most sought after product. We even have less resources in promotion and advertising as we have to rely upon our own capabilities.

With hard work and prayers, we made it to the top. (Prayers are great weapons in all times).

Teamwork.

This is a Filipino company, ran and managed by Filipinos.

Keeping the morale of the workforce high and enhancing their faith and confidence in the Filipino capability, value, and innate goodness have been daily menu.

I have to inspire every employee because my strength lies in our unity. To break ranks could give my competitors an advantage. And worst, it would erode the goal of nurturing a company with the spirit of "Filipino-ness" in it. It would mean that Filipinos can't make it on their own. That they are colonial-minded and undisciplined. That foreigners must rule them and that they're proud and happy in that atmosphere. This consensus I cannot accept.

I assure you,

though, that the road to success we have taken is longer, harder, and thornier.

Others may find monetary success in a few years through shortcuts and special deals. The Solid Corporation road, though strewn with difficulties, trials, frustrations, and many times mixed with tears of anxiety and hopelessness, has come through because of a deep sense of fulfillment and a strong belief in God's will.

You see, it is not how fast we reach our goal that counts. It is how we reach it. Then at the end of our lives we can face our Maker and say that we did our best according to His way.

His way means to endure, to persist, to keep faith, to be true, not to cause injury to anyone. It is not quantifiable.

But to do it His way is a delightful joy, a silent song, a tender glow, a flower spraying fragrance into the air, a bird in flight.

It is a mysterious kind

of happiness that the spirit is eternally free and not trapped in lead, iron, silver, or gold. It is the knowledge that God will accept our offering. All our deeds are done for His glory. The more difficult and thorny the road, the greater the gift.

Chapter Three

Black Tiger Prawn

RIDING
THE TIGER
TO SUCCESS

Few people know it but the Philippines holds the distinct honor of being the first country to develop and promote the black tiger prawn ("sugpo" in Pilipino) to the international market, particularly Japan.

This was achieved through the pioneering efforts of AA Export and Import Corporation (AA), a member of the Solid Group of Companies.

Before 1975, the export of Philippine sea-catch prawns was an infant industry which generated barely US$5 million per year for the Philippines. But as a result of AA's innovation of introducing the black tiger prawn variety to the Japanese market, followed by its aggressive production and marketing program, for the past decade the industry has averaged US$250 million of annual export receipts for the Philippine economy.

Many other Southeast Asian countries have followed the Philippine example and now, the region has made tremendous exports with foreign exchange earnings exceeding US$5 BILLION annually.

A casual remark,

coupled with a nagging problem, started our black tiger prawn story.

The problem was an unproductive piece of land in Balut, Tondo, Manila which I had acquired in 1959. I did not relish the thought of paying taxes on it year-in and year-out, when only unauthorized dwellers had use of the land. I had racked my mind over what was best to do, but to no avail.

Then, one evening in 1971, I attended a dinner party given by my friend, erstwhile Canadian Ambassador Frank Clark. He showed me what seemed like a block of ice except that inside the block were frozen shrimps.

"You're so lucky," I exclaimed with perhaps a tinge of surprise, "you have imported wine, imported canned goods, and now, even imported shrimps!"

"Canadian shrimps?" Frank chuckled. "But Elena, these are frozen shrimps actually processed and packed here in the Philippines."

It was a casual remark which I could have dismissed with a shrug and forgotten in the gaiety of the evening. But thank God, his casual remark touched a spark in me. I could just have gone on thinking Frank was one lucky fellow and let it go at that. Instead, I asked him more questions about the shrimps which he readily answered. I learned that the shrimps were being exported by a certain Mr. Kwong, a Filipino businessman.

Processed shrimps for export?

The thought held a world of meaning for me. It clung to me throughout the party. I kept asking myself if it wasn't the answer to my problem concerning the idle piece of land in Balut, Tondo, which was eating so much real estate tax money.

I never even entertained the thought that exporting processed shrimps might be an impossible dream. We didn't have the knowledge to start a business like that of Mr. Kwong's. I dared to envision my Tondo piece of land as a processing plant for shrimps to be exported later on. I was solving an immediate problem. I did not allow myself any qualms. I wasn't bothered with what was to come later. I dreamed, but I did not stop there. I worked to bring that dream to reality.

When an idea

takes hold of me, I do not allow it to grow stale. I immediately set things in motion towards the fruition of my idea. Thus, after having stumbled, so to speak, on what to me was the solution to my problem of the idle Tondo land, I sought the opinion of my family and friends. Gaining their approval, I entered into a venture which I knew nothing about . . . export of shrimps and prawns.

Actually, there were no experts

then. Since the industry was in its infancy, everyone was basically learning the ropes.

True, there were shrimp processors ahead of AA, such as Mr. Kwong, but they did business irregularly and in negligible quantities.

The ones involved in the business were chiefly the fishermen, the trawler operators, and the fishpond owners. Their business, however, was circumstantial, not intentional. The fishermen's shrimp catch was incidental, a minimal part of their fishing venture.

As for the fishpond operators, their prawns were just a secondary crop, next to milkfish ("*bangus*" in Pilipino, considered the "national cultured fish"). They had prawns whenever they harvested milkfish from their ponds. The operations and production of shrimps and prawns in those days were therefore seasonal.

There was also quite a number of fly-by-night operators disrupting the erratic flow of legitimate business when AA came into the scene. These fly-by-night operators were those without permanent business addresses. They simply brought their shrimps to any cold storage plant to process their shrimps under unhygienic and substandard conditions, thus producing shrimps of very inferior quality and actually carrying a very poor image of Philippine shrimps in the international market.

In hindsight,

I believe that I plunged our resources into the rough uncharted sea of the shrimp and prawn business not just because it was the first ready solution to my land tax problem, but because the pioneer spirit in me was intrigued by the possibilities opened to me by Mr. Clark's remark. As far as I was concerned, it was far better to risk the hazards of pioneering a business with great export potential than to enter the arena of an aging business with so many competitors. There seemed a great opportunity here waiting to be tapped.

Anyway, it was a challenge and I lost no time in registering the new business with the Securities and Exchange Commission. The plant was set up on the land after I had the unauthorized dwellers relocated with some financial assistance, in keeping with our Filipino culture. As for the company name, we borrowed from one of our earliest ventures. And so, AA EXPORT AND IMPORT CORPORATION was incorporated in 1971.

I was certainly relieved

to see my Tondo property being cleared and prepared for the shrimp processing plant. The difficulties were yet to come. Since we were plunging blindly into the unknown, our ignorance was bliss at the time or else we may have balked at continuing with the project. Just the same, all five members of our Board of Directors were determined to make the project succeed. On top of the project was George Tan, an engineer by study and an entrepreneur by choice.

A modest building was put up to house the processing plant and business office of AA Export and Import Corporation. Construction of the building and installation of facilities and equipment took all of two years.

The streets of Manila

were then the scenes of prevailing political unrest. The year 1971 was the prelude to Martial Law in 1972 and rallies and demonstrations were daily fare.

On September 21, 1972, President Marcos imposed Martial Law. The business sector was fraught with grim foreboding. We experienced initial qualms although our plant was almost ready for operation.

But entrepreneurs must have the courage

to take risks and follow their business instincts. So we decided to continue with the construction of our plant.

On May 28, 1973, AA Export and Import Corp. opened its doors for business, starting very modestly with 12 shrimp processors and an office staff of four.

Japan was clearly the

ideal market for AA's shrimps and prawns. Two reasons: First, it is the world's biggest importing market for shrimps and prawns. Second, it is very near to us — a fundamental consideration especially for exports of perishable goods.

We had set our initial shipment to Japan at ten tons. I was banking on using our Japanese contacts: Mitsubishi Corporation and Toyo Menka Kaisha, Ltd., both "sogo-sosha" firms; and even Sony Corporation.

Mitsubishi was an old trading partner. Through them we imported products for our other ventures like synthetic resins, all kinds of sheet glass, as well as some other goods and machinery.

Our first major problem
in selling the black tiger prawn was the prawn itself.

Japanese consumers then were really repulsed by the black tiger prawn. They were not familiar with the specie since it is not found in Japanese waters. Besides, they considered the color black as dirty and unappealing.

No amount of praise of the black tiger's superb taste and quality could overcome their prejudice. They had become so used to the pink, white and even brown variety of raw shrimps that look attractive.

The black tiger prawn comes from milkfish ponds and its color is truly black. This is due to the black water environment in the milkfish ponds.

Our dilemma
then was that even though the black tiger prawn's color was unattractive, unappealing, and totally unacceptable to the Japanese buyers, it is the only prawn specie available in the Philippines that can be processed fresh because the time gap between its harvest (from milkfish ponds) and processing is but a matter of hours. Therefore, when we process this particular prawn specie which arrives fresh — even alive, at times — in our plant, the finished

product for export is of excellent quality.

On the other hand, the other prawn species like the pink, brown, yellow and white coming from the sea catch, usually had already been inundated in ice for several days before they arrived in our processing plant. The time gap hastened their deterioration, causing soft shell, broken antennae, broken heads or tail and soft-damaged body. No amount of good freezing equipment or excellent work force can ever produce good quality shrimps for export if the basic raw materials are inferior or of poor quality.

This was a big headache

especially during our first two years. Like the rest of the processors then, AA bought its shrimps from the fishermen, the trawlers and traders at the wholesale market. Almost always, the black tiger prawns were unavoidably mixed with the ordinary sea-catch shrimp purchases. In such instances, our Japanese buyers would immediately lodge their complaints.

"George," Kanasawa, our distributor in Japan would call, "your shipment contained some black shrimps, huh? Black shrimps mixed with flower and uh . . . in some blocks. We receive complaints from customers. Please ask girl sorter, huh . . . be little more careful not to include black with regular sea catch shrimps. OKs huh?"

"Oh, so sorry, Mr. Kana," George would reply, "but black colored shrimps are very tasty . . . highly prized and more expensive . . . "

"Maybe true," Kanazawa would cut him short, "but uh . . . Japanese . . . uh . . . consumers here very particular . . . yes, very particular about appearance. They don't accept ugly black-looking prawn."

A feeling of waste would spread in AA each time we were informed of these rejections. The complaints and demand of our distributors were getting to be too frequent for our comfort. It was problematic that these prawns that were highly prized here in the Philippines were unacceptable over there in Japan.

It was only later that we learned how true Mr. Kanazawa and Mr. Aoki's objections were.

We determined to do all we could think of to change their attitude towards the black tiger prawn. The Japanese market became a challenge.

Shrimps are distinguished from prawns

by their inconspicuous rostrum or beak which is radically different from the serrated long rostrum of the prawns. In form shrimps are long and tapering, with an arched abdomen giving them a hunchback appearance. In common application there is consensus that shrimps do not differ much from prawns.

We can lightly say that a shrimp is a small prawn, and a prawn is a large shrimp . . . except that prawns are much darker in color. In fact, a special specie of prawn is black . . . the black tiger prawn.

Then we also made a major blunder

in our choice of freezing equipment.

Owing to our lack of technical expertise in production and freezing techniques, added to a misdirected altruistic desire to patronize Filipino-built freezing equipment,we allowed a local freezing equipment maker to install his own locally designed freezer in our plant, not knowing he had the wrong technology in trying to use local materials and reconditioned parts to make a low temperature freezing equipment. One must remember that shrimps and prawns are delicate and valuable seafood. They must be kept firm and fresh as soon as they are harvested from the sea or the ponds.

Our supplier thought

that our requirements were similar to the local need, good enough for normal refrigeration up to zero degree centigrade. He didn't realize that as soon as the shrimps and prawns are harvested from the sea or the ponds, the temperature needed was minus 40 degrees centigrade so as to keep them well frozen, since bacteria does not multiply in such freezing temperature.

The locally-made freezing machine froze only the surface and the bottom of the ice block. Inside the ice block, the shrimps weren't frozen at all. Thus, when thawed, the shrimps turned out totally spoiled and emitted a bad odor. Furthermore, the machine took 24 hours to freeze the half-frozen blocks.

That mistake caused us much anxiety and losses. Instead of exporting our much awaited good quality prawns, we ended up selling our shrimps and prawns to the local market as "hebi" or dried shrimps.

We incurred unrecoverable production expenses and unrealized projected income. It certainly seemed the worst of times and the best time to quit.

Government was another big problem.

This was in the seventies, under the martial law administration of President Ferdinand Marcos.

Our government was shortsighted, not realizing the value of the shrimp exporters' contribution to the economy. Our policymakers who were so engrossed with looking for ways to raise revenues missed the answer which was right under their noses: Support the country's aqua farmers and exporters because much of a country's income grows in tandem with the export industry.

A huge share of government funds was spent on projects like the Philippine International Convention Center, Philippine Folks Arts Theater, Miss Universe pageant, the Manila Film Center, and other similar "white elephant" projects of the Philippine Tourism Authority.

On the other hand, Asian countries like Thailand, Taiwan and Indonesia supported their exporters by giving them long-term loans which carried interest rates as low as 4% to 4.5% annually, as well as long-term lease payments.

These were the incentives that we Filipino exporters wished we had from our government. Instead, the incentives given us were, at best, mainly in the form of reduced income tax and duty and tax free importation of capital equipment.

To avail of such incentives, the exporter had to be registered with the BOI. The process of registering, however, was oftentimes burdensome, costly and time-consuming, discouraging several firms engaged in the shrimp and prawn business from registration.

The few of us who registered with the BOI experienced periodic problems due to the lack of agreement on policies among the different government departments. Incentives given us by the BOI which I considered as the government's right hand were oftentimes snatched from us in one breath by the Ministry of Finance, the government's left hand.

The tax burdens from 1975-1979

stunted the growth of the shrimp export industry. Our poor performance impelled me to rally all the members of the Shrimp Exporters Association of the Philippines (SHRIMPEX) to lobby for the abolition of the 4% export tax of freight on board (FOB) value of exports and inspection fee of 1/2% of the FOB value.

We believe that taxing 4% on export of shrimps is untenable. As to the inspection fee, it should not be based on percentage of value, but on a flat amount commensurate to the inspection activity. Aside from this, we still have to get clearance from the Food and Drug Adminstration (FDA). So the inspection fee is even duplicating FDA work.

SHRIMPEX filed with the BOI a formal complaint arguing that these taxes were offensive and unfair. The BOI agreed with our rationale and discussed the matter with the Ministry Of Justice. The tax-happy Ministry of Finance remained adamant in its position. Not to be outdone, the Bureau Of Fisheries and Aquatic Resources (BFAR) slapped an additional fee of 5% of the FOB value of exports at a certain period aside from the other taxes and fees such as income tax, licenses, and collection fees.

It was a fee-hungry period, indeed. Revenue was the goal, not the development of the industry. This proved to be a shortsighted policy because in the long run, we lost more.

All these impositions curtailed our business without let-up for a considerable duration. It was a relief to learn months later that this 5% BFAR fee was removed. However, the inspection fee of 1/2 of 1% of the FOB value of exports remained.

These lackadaisical changes in policies demonstrated the haphazard trial-and-error methods applied by the government in its misguided scrounging for sources of national funds.

We also faced the problem

of dealing with "sogo soshas." These were the Japanese trading houses an exporter usually had to go through to penetrate the Japanese market.

The determination of AA to hang on in bad as well as in good times attracted the attention of these Japanese importers. Toyo Menka which had been studying local production approached AA to be their exclusive distributor. We refused the offer. Instead, we entered into a contract that limited Toyo Menka to being AA's distributor only in Japan with a clinching clause that the Japanese market would continuously absorb AA products throughout the year at fairly competitive prices.

This agreement lasted for a while until such factors as pricing and volume difficulty compounded by irregular influx of orders set in. Nonetheless, we must admit that Toyo Menka proved to be a helpful business contact. It even employed one of its agents to further train and teach AA personnel the techniques in prawn processing.

Another Japanese wholesale distributor, Tohto Suisan Co., Ltd., sent over a group of technicians to update AA's processing techniques. Mitsui Norin, still another trading house, also lent its experts. With the help of these Japanese technicians AA was able to set its own international standard requirement of proper handling, sorting, sizing, freezing, and packing of prawn products. To the Japanese market, AA became the model processing plant in the Philippines. And it was this model processing plant that our distributors saw when we brought them over during the promotional and marketing campaign for the black tiger prawn.

While the Japanese trading houses had been helpful in upgrading AA's quality standards they also presented us with certain disadvantages. For example, a change in their executives sometimes spelled total change in policies. Our good relations with the former would vanish as quickly as new executives with different policies would step in and carry on the business with their own brand of management.

This was exactly what happened with the Tokyo trading company we developed. The new CE0 decided to shift priorities to the fish roe business, thus relegating shrimp and prawn to a lesser priority. Clearly, our marketing setup in Japan was far from ideal when we were just dealing with the trading houses.

AA lacked a good set of focused outlets that would be faithful to our brand. Choice consumers such as hotels, restaurant chains, clubs and such institutions were unaware of our brand because of the indiscriminate mixing of our product with other brands.

As though these problems weren't enough, the world export prices plummeted beyond control. The oil crises of the period brought down prices to a level below our cost. This kept us holding on to our inventory hoping that the price would recover. But instead of recovering, the prices plummeted more and more until we were finally forced to sell at 50% below our production cost.

AA nevertheless plodded on. Financial losses mounted especially as AA at the time was forced to rent other cold storage facilities due to the faulty freezer and lack of cold storage facilities suited for shrimps and prawns.

AA's original capital was already wiped out by this time, and bank loan payments were fast getting overdue.

This roller-coaster trend of the business left us bewildered and spurred us to look for other market opportunities to bridge the huge losses. The world market went haywire. Many fishing boats were lying idle and Japanese import prices plunged, discouraging many shrimp suppliers from continuing with fishing. At this time, many big fishing companies went bankrupt and had their vessels taken over by banks.

To compound the disaster,

AA speculated that the situation would improve and that prices would soon climb upward. So we filled our storage with frozen stock. But the speculated climb did not happen. In fact, import prices plunged even much lower. Stunned, we were forced to sell our huge stock at a loss. Again, AA teetered on bankruptcy.

Talks of closure

to avoid greater loss circulated in the plant, affecting morale. But I would not hear of it. I simply couldn't accept defeat, not when I was at the helm of the business. The word "failure" is not part of my vocabulary. Opportunity and challenge are. The situation was just another challenge to prove my mettle. As my favorite poem *Invictus* says, "... *my head is bloody but unbowed ...*" It is a poem I recommend to every entrepreneur.

There'll be times when you'll find yourself embattled but you should not give up without putting up a good fight. But you must also remember to learn from mistakes, quickly correct and not repeat them. Continued improvement is a cardinal rule.

First thing in my survival kit

was to put additional capital into the company.

Next, I acted on a long-delayed decision to order a new one-ton contact freezer from Japan. I had given the manufacturer of the faulty freezer ample time to improve his locally assembled machinery but he did not come up with anything better. So he had no cause to gripe when I ordered the offensive freezer thrown out of the factory.

The new freezer tremendously enhanced AA's business horizon. So I ordered another. AA's processed shrimps came out beautifully and were well preserved. With the two contact freezers AA crept out of the red slowly but surely.

AA's tenacity

and capacity to stay on course despite the rough sailing amazed Gov. Conrado Sanchez of the BOI. "Elena," he exclaimed, "others are shying away from this business, yet here you are, aggressively going into it."

"That's just the cycle of life," I told him. "When one leaves, another takes his place."

I did not bother to tell him how we had to sink in more money in the business so as not to lose money. Paradoxical, wouldn't you say? The contact freezers were quite expensive and an apparent drain on our budget — but the returns were more than satisfactory. AA had recovered from imminent bankruptcy.

Creative and courageous problem-solving

is a basic requirement for any entrepreneur.

For the problem of Japanese resistance to the black tiger prawn, I told George Tan: "It is essential to convince our distributors first. Let's show them the potential of the black tiger prawn as a gourmet food in Japanese restaurants hotels and consequently, in Japanese households."

"I'm with you," George assured me. "Time will come when AA's Black Tiger will find its respectable place on Japanese tables. It will soon be a Japanese preference." How prophetic indeed were the words of George. Today, the black tiger prawn is a preferred specie.

We carefully mapped out our strategy. Filipino

hospitality was high on our list of promotional blitz. We premised our strategy on the axiom that a picture is worth more than a thousand words . . . ergo, we said, the real thing must be worth more than a thousand pictures.

So we arranged

for our Japanese distributors to be treated to a sightseeing tour of our AA facilities in addition to the usual tourist itinerary of historic sites and other tourism come-ons. We believed that the sight of our plants and of our working force would give our distributors a deeper sense of involvement and confidence and thus spur them on to better promote our products, especially the black tiger prawn.

Having mapped out our strategy we proceeded to fly at company expense our Japanese distributors. AA shouldered not just their travel but also all accommodation expenses. Needless to say, the distributors were charmed by the warmth and lavish hospitality of our country and people. Many of them went home to return later with their families and friends at their own expense. Our tourism industry profited from AA's promotional tours.

Cooking sessions were the highlight

of our promotional blitz. The axiom on which we based our strategy proved right. The whole campaign focused on the best qualities of the black tiger prawns: its glossy hard shell, firm delicious meat, and bigger-than-average shrimp size.

AA therefore arranged for cooking sessions to the amazement and delight of our captive audience: the distributors. They were very surprised to see that after being cooked, the color of the black tiger prawn turned into a beautiful red — the prevailing appearance that their customers wanted. These demos were duplicated in many sessions in Tokyo.

For our Tokyo campaign

aimed at the end-buyers themselves, I remember an incredulous George Tan asking: "You really mean to do the cooking?"

"Yes, we will," was my simple answer.

There's nothing like one's personal attention to ensure success in a delicate operation. So George and I, together with other AA distributors, donned aprons and cook's caps and proceeded to cook black tiger prawns under the noses of our potential Japanese customers. Oohs . . . and ahh . . . ahh filled the air as our Japanese audience, wide-eyed, witnessed for themselves the abhorred black-colored prawns turn to a delicious looking red-colored prawn dish.

Just as we expected, when the mouth-watering sweet aroma of cooking prawns permeated the atmosphere, our potential customers became even more excited. It was exhilarating to see them impatiently waiting for the taste of the "sugpo" as we peeled off the shells from the cooked prawns to reveal even redder, juicier prawn meat. Again . . . Oh . . . ooh . . . mmm . . . mmm filled the air as they savored the delectable seafood, sampling piece after piece.

Having witnessed the success of our demonstrations, our Japanese distributors eagerly extracted a promise from AA that they would be provided a regular supply of prawns. AA, on the other hand made them promise to commit themselves to the AA brand and to actively handle its promotion with resourcefulness and loyalty.

For two years, this vigorous campaign for the

acceptance of the black tiger prawn in Japan was carried on.

The acceptance

of the black tiger prawn in the Japanese market was certainly a monumental breakthrough for the Philippine export business.

The volume of shipment of the black tiger prawns from the Philippines to Japan began to rise dramatically in 1977 and reached a peak in 1979. After a slight decline in 1980, the volume resumed with a slow ascent. Philippine exports attained a volume of over 20,000 metric tons in 1987 and was projected to grow 30%-40% annually over the next five years. Unfortunately, this projection did not take place.

To solve the problem of dealing

with highly unpredictable Japanese trading houses, upon the suggestion of our Japanese contacts we developed a special group of distributors to promote and distribute our AA brand of shrimps and prawns exclusively. Without this strategy we would have suffered more and the promotion blitz as well as the sales campaign that we initiated to promote our product in Japan would have been set back.

A list of probable candidates for distributorship was given to us by Messrs. Essuhara Kanasawa and Hideaki Aoki of Tohto Suisan. Mr. Hiroshi Asano of Mitsui Morin did likewise.

George Tan had to make several trips to Japan to meet the prospective "AA TOKYO GROUP" wholesalers who were to be our exclusive distributors in Japan. Finally, the choice was limited to 12 but one bowed out later so we had 11. They were:

AA TOKYO GROUP

1. AA MARISCOS CORPORATION
    Hideaki Hoki - President
    Kasuhara Kanasawa - Sales Managing Director

2. COOP TRADE JAPAN, LTD.
    Shunji Tsuboi - President

3. EBIJYO & CO., LTD.
    Yasuo Ogawa - Director & Manager

4. TOHTO & ISAN CO., LTD.
    Hiroshige Nakamura

5. ISHIKAWA SHOTEN CO., LTD.
    Shiroshi Ishikawa - President

6. KATO PRODUCT CO., LTD.
    Horihiro Kato - President

7. MARUSADA COMPANY, LTD.
    Masahiko Tokudoh - President

8. UNO CO., LTD.
    Hiroyuki Nakano

9. DAIROKU BUNTEN CO., LTD.
    Oshiyuki Senga

10. TSUKURIN CO., LTD.

Shunsaka Kawasaki

11. KISHIGAMI CO., LTD.
Tiruo Kishigami

The AA Mariscos Corporation
was organized in Tokyo with an initial capitalization of two million (2,000,000) Japanese yen.

The shift in the AA marketing network meant that the "AA members" were to conduct business with AA Mariscos instead of the usual trading houses which had become of no use to us since their new officials preferred other kinds of seafood to shrimps and prawns, plus the fact that the orders they placed with us were very erratic, especially when demand for prawns dwindled. They were also not fully committed to our brand.

Our group of eleven worked hard to sell and promote the AA brand of shrimps and prawns. As a result AA, was on the roster of prime shrimp and prawn exporters in Japan. We rated sixth in the list of that period (1980-1985).

This special group was also responsible for laying the solid foundation for the success of the entire black tiger prawn industry in world trade. They deserve due recognition and honor for their exemplary marketing achievement.

As our AA experience has shown, mutual cooperation is a very important element of trade success. This bond between AA and the AA Group (Tokyo) based on harmonious cooperation and respect has endured up to the present.

What had started as a strictly business partnership has now evolved into a higher level of friendship slowly bordering on personal family relationship.

The secret lies in trusting delegation of power and responsibility from the authority figure to persons with competence, virtue, innovation, intelligence, and dynamism.

I have always been a strong advocate of the principle of delegating power to the "rightman." This "rightman" will map out a system within the framework of the corporate plan and philosophy which has been formulated. This to me is the key to nurturing highly efficient and excellent managers.

Of course, I create and develop the basic guidelines and policies of the company around a single corporate thought from which stems the system of management responsibility as the organization grows. This is done with full consensus of the company executives and board members. Organizational success however does not rest on one man's shoulders but on the collective efforts of all who are part of the organization. In our export success on black tiger prawns, I acknowledge humbly and candidly the help and dedication of our Japanese distributors especially Messrs. Kanasawa and Aoki.

Another problem we had to solve

was how to avail of a consistent volume of supply of shrimps in order to maintain a stable export volume.

To do this, the idea that entered our minds was *expansion*. A big expansion plan that included a prawn hatchery, a grow-out pond operations, and opening new international markets in the United States and Europe.

Why not? I told myself. AA was already experiencing a modest profitable period due to the hefty boost given by the Japanese market to our annual sales and profits. This was in the late seventies. I knew it was time for expanding AA's business operations.

We were not acting on pure instinct alone. We had heard of a non-operating ice plant for sale in Roxas City, Capiz (a province in Panay Island).

According to information,

the plant had been abandoned and thieves had done away with all machinery and equipment.

That didn't faze us because we believed that Roxas City in Panay Island was a very good site for raising prawns in ponds.

We also had faith in the prawn as a very valuable dollar-earning seafood product.

Above all, we believed that with proper management of its operations added to the advantage of a firm tie-up with our then twelve Tokyo distributors, the abandoned plant could be renovated to become productive.

So we expanded to the Visayas Region. Southward we sallied forth to meet with the Japanese manager in charge of the abandoned plant. However, it turned out that the office was in Makati, Metro Manila.

Nisho Iwai was happy

to finally meet a serious buyer for the long abandoned plant.

During the course of our negotiations, however, I found out that there were other owners and that the majority of stock belonged to the Lim brothers. They were the Filipino owners and they were the decision-makers: Manny and Victor Lim. So I met with Victor Lim.

Victor informed me that Nisho Iwai was not an owner; he was their creditor. He supplied the as-yet-unpaid machinery to their plant. Asked why the company went bankrupt, Victor Lim enumerated several reasons:

⊕ Erratic shrimp supply because their source was the seasonal sea-catch;

⊕ High cost of transporting the frozen shrimps from Roxas City to the Manila International Airport (MIA);

⊕ Poor quality shrimps due to the absence of refrigerated vans to pick up crates of shrimps; thus, the shrimps were unloaded on the ground with the sun bearing down on them for sometime before they could be placed in any refrigerated storage; and

⊕ Their buyer and manager in Roxas were sourcing shrimps at high prices, and didn't have the skill for mass production.

Incurring losses, the Lim brothers had the plant closed, with only a guard to watch over it. But according to George Tan who had gone to inspect the property, the plant was abandoned and cannibalized by thieves. George also informed me that the plant was not worth the price they were asking for it.

"Forget this plant,"

George said. "We can put up a new one for less than their asking price."

Over several cups of coffee, however, I discussed terms and conditions of the sale with Victor Lim. I asked him if he had seen the present condition of the plant he was selling at such a price. After all I had seen the plant already and knew that it wasn't worth the price they were quoting. Nevertheless, sensing that the Lim brothers were like their father, our former Secretary Of Commerce, Manuel Lim, Sr., men of integrity, I asked him to reconsider his price after he had evaluated the value of its present asset.

"Have you seen the condition of the plant now?" I asked.

"No," he confessed, "I haven't been there in a long time."

"Why don't you go there first and see for yourself how much it is really worth," I encouraged him.

As I expected,

after he had sent his men to make an ocular inspection and submit a factual report about the long-abandoned and cannibalized plant, he offered me a very reasonable price. We concluded the deal to our mutual satisfaction. Was I elated! I was happy when I told George over the phone: "We've got it! The plant is ours. Go and see what we need there. Get it done quickly. Let's give it life."

The incident shows negotiation is made easier when it is made between people who are friendly towards each other. I would advise the would-be entrepreneur-negotiator to know as many people as possible and develop friendship and goodwill so that even just over a cup or two of coffee, one can easily come to terms with other parties.

The speedy sale happened, I must also say, because of the professionalism and integrity of the brothers Manny and Victor Lim. If their shrimp processing plant failed it was because they put it up when the industry was still in its infancy, not to mention the other contributing factors earlier mentioned. Thus they found selling to the international market tough as we have experienced.

Nevertheless, the pioneering venture of the Lim brothers remains not only as their contribution to the Philippine shrimp and prawn industry but also as a symbol of Filipino entrepreneurial spirit for the nation's benefit. Today, that plant has been totally demolished. On the same ground now stands a very modern and new shrimp processing plant with the best freezing equipment and cold storage facilities.

"Elena," I remember Mr. Lim saying, "if it weren't for you, I would not have sold it. I'm glad you bought it because I know you'll breathe life into it for the good of the people of Roxas."

Well, we got the Roxas plant

and it was as if we asked for hard work. Real hard work. Nonetheless, I relished the vision of AA's entry into the production side of the prawn export industry. I was eager to go into the hatchery and grow-out ponds operations using Japanese technology. We were eager to learn from their technology which George and I witnessed in Kagoshima, Japan, where we visited a highly productive grow out pond operation plant.

It was an incredible sight to see the application of high technology in processing fresh shrimps. The shrimps that were being harvested from the ponds were quickly rendered unconscious by electrical shock then packed inside boxes lined with pine leaves. By this method, the shrimps remain alive up to seven days in cool temperature. Once the box is opened, the shrimps jump up alive!

This type of operation is done remarkably well in Japan and the product commands a very high price. However, we couldn't raise live shrimps considering its limited market, as well as the short life span of such shrimps. Nonetheless, our newly bought plant in Roxas intended for processing black tiger prawns in block was already accepted in Japan.

Roxas City was an excellent

choice of venue because of the abundance of milkfish ponds

and marine catch around its area. We intended to complement these available resources by putting up our own hatchery of prawn fry. It was our way of creating a symbolic tie between AA and the local fishpond owners. AA would buy their harvest of prawns and in return they could buy prawn fry from AA. Already in my mind there was a vision of these milkfish ponds being transformed into prawn ponds. Again let me stress that this was way back in the late seventies to early eighties.

We could not complain when we saw the sorry remnant of a building that we intended to be our processing plant in Roxas city. It had been an as-is-where-is sale. Anyway what mattered most to me was the site. But truly, it was most disheartening to see how thieves had vandalized the plant. Its walls and roofs bore marks of vandalism. Its machinery and equipment were stripped and gutted of parts, and the wiring system was nowhere to be found.

Thus AA hastily began restoration of plant facilities. Only our enthusiasm on gaining a favorable site and our determination to carry our expansion plans allowed us to take in stride the arduous task of rehabilitating the broken-down plant.

Feverishly we repaired,
replaced, and built new structures.

The ice-plant was reconstructed and two brand-new contact freezers were installed.

Since water is needed to process shrimps, AA also had to dig a well. Unfortunately, no fresh water would come up from the well. AA had to construct a huge water reservoir and buy two tankers to transport water from the town to our site. It goes without saying that this was another of those to-be-expected unexpected expenses an entrepreneur must be prepared for.

In addition to these alternatives to solving the absence of water in the site, AA had to purchase a piece of land in the town to build a well from which water could be drawn.

It was also necessary to repair and widen the road leading to the plant which was narrow, unpaved, and dotted with mini-craters and overgrown weeds. It was a poor excuse for a road.

There seemed no end to our problems and huge financial disbursements. Having solved the problem of water supply, we were then faced with the problem of electrical connections. There was simply no connection to the town source. We had to buy two sets of generators; one for regular use, the other to serve as a stand-by unit in case of mechanical trouble. This foresight was to prove a boon later.

While all these renovations

and construction were going on, George Tan was kept busy hiring new employees, being endowed with the knack for choosing the right people to train as future leaders and supervisors, most of whom are now the trusted and highly regarded members of the AA family. Mr. Raffy del Rosario is one such employee hand-picked by George to manage the Roxas farm.

In November 1978, the Roxas farm was declared open for operations.

George Tan flew in from Manila to oversee the start of operations.

Day 1. No one came in.

Since no one came in with shrimp catch, there was no

shrimp to process.

Day 2 was no better although someone came in a tricycle with one pail of shrimps. That was all they had to process for the day. George comforted Raffy, the manager, by telling him that things would soon get better. Within himself, though, he wondered how, if ever.

On the third day, George tried to convince a fishpond owner to harvest. The man hedged, giving all sorts of excuses for not harvesting: it was untimely, prices were not right, and the like.

George persisted in talking not just to one but to every fishpond owner he could talk to, persuading them to harvest and bring in their harvest for processing. The fourth day brought in a little more than one pail of shrimps but not enough to justify having a processing plant that cost us so much.

But the fifth day was different. George's persistence paid off. The total yield was one ton. Was George pleased and surprised!

It was the start

of the many frenzied activities to make the Roxas plant the model shrimp processing plant of the country. From that time on we had to charter from five to six plane flights from Roxas to Manila. We had all the supply we could handle. There was a time when we had to charter a C-130 plane . . . the same type of plane the Israelis used to raid Entebbe.

We were spending so much for chartering and loading that when we calculated the costs we found out that we could have bought our own plane with what we had spent. Consequently, we purchased two boats for transporting the shrimps and prawns from Roxas to Manila.

George christened the two boats as "Doña Elena I" and "Doña Elena II." I objected to the use of my name especially with the "Doña" prefix which is alien to my humble beginnings and my character. But my objections came too late. The names had been registered and painted on the boats. Later on, the volume of supply necessitated buying three more boats.

With the Roxas plant in full operation we focused our attention to the local sources of shrimps and prawns. AA deemed very timely the forging of our partnership with AA Mariscos, Corp., Mitsui Norin, and Coop Trade Japan, Ltd., in 1979 for purposes of distributing and marketing of AA products, particularly the black tiger prawn.

Our participation in the agreement
was to provide these corporations a sizable steady volume of quality shrimps and prawns regularly. Towards this end we decided to enter into the prawn monoculture. To achieve this, we organized a spin-off operation called the AA Marine Development Corporation or MADECO.

With the three companies in Japan providing the technology, AA MADECO devoted its operations to prawn farming. The firm was originally registered with the BOI on a pioneer status hatchery. From this pilot farm, several small and medium-sized hatcheries proliferated throughout the country.

This new venture earned instant success because the members of the technical staff were allowed to implement their own innovations in the process. Soon AA MADECO was selling prawn fry to the fishpond operators of Roxas City. Excellent technology and harmonious relationship between the company and the fishpond operators spelled success for the prawn export industry.

When word spread

about the initial success of MADECO, several entrepreneurs were inspired to embark on the same business. We generously opened our doors to all who desired to do so. San Miguel Corporation, an industrial giant, put up its own hatchery and processing plant in Calatrava.

Soon after, Mr. Eduardo Cojuangco, then Chairman of San Miguel Corporation (the largest Filipino food and beverage company), developed the same project in Malita, Davao.

We trained their workers in our Roxas plant and sent our supervisors to assist them in their own operations. From the eighties to the early nineties, everybody wanted to get involved in the prawn business. AA was gratified to watch the industry grow.

From a greenhorn in the underdeveloped prawn industry in 1973, AA has consistently landed in the roster of the country's "Top 1,000 Corporations" for having charted the course of the industry to its phenomenal growth. Slowly but surely, AA inched its way up the ladder of success notwithstanding the crisis in the Philippine economy.

Not all was smooth sailing,

though. There were problems, of course, and we had to cope with them the best we could.

I am reminded of an incident that now may be viewed as an anecdote but which, at the time, was truly worrisome. Were it not for the goodwill we had invested it would have meant the loss of a regular customer and, perhaps, the loss of business for one of our distributors.

Lead was discovered inside the black

tiger prawns delivered by one of our distributors in Japan to a 5-star hotel for a wedding reception.

The cook who discovered it was very alarmed. He called up our distributor to complain of the anomalous delivery and to demand an explanation.

Without calling us up our Japanese distributor took it upon himself to replace the offensive prawns double the quantity. He also instructed the cook to return the lead-filled prawns.

Only then did he call us up to tell us of how he had averted what would given our AA brand a blackeye in Japan. We could do no less than prove true to his trust in us: we reimbursed the entire cost of the offensive delivery and the double-portion replacement. Indeed, goodwill's trust and cooperation played important roles in that situation.

Of course, we did not leave the matter just like that.

Upon careful investigation,

we traced the source of the offending supply to our Leyte plant.

Hoping to get a better price for his prawns, the supplier inserted lead in the bellies of the prawns to increase their weight. Thus he was paid more for delivering less.

Our investigators also found out that at times, slivers of bamboo would be inserted into the prawns' necks to firm up the heads, because head-on prawns and shrimps were valued more than headless prawns and shrimps.

These forms of cheating were confined to a certain section in Leyte province, probably due to extreme poverty in that depressed and underdeveloped region. Ironically, it is the home province of the former First Lady, Imelda Marcos, and mine as well.

We took stringent measures to prevent the reoccurrence of such offensive and abhorrent practices among our suppliers. As a remedial measure, we purchased a metal-detector machine similar to the kind found in airports that departing passengers have to pass through. We installed it in our Leyte plant to detect metal substances in the shrimps and prawns delivered to us. This proved to be a strong deterrent because the practice has stopped.

It saddens me, however, to think that our fisherman-suppliers would resort to such unconscionable acts, not realizing that they are destroying the very business that benefits them.

New problems cropped up.

While a volatile economic crisis plagued the entire business sector in 1984, the government slapped a 30% stabilisation tax on all exports from the Philippines with the outright exemption of the multinationals engaged in the manufacture of semi-conductors.

All other exporters including shrimp and prawn exporters had to comply with this new tax regulation. It clearly revealed our government's discrimination against the small business sectors who had no clout at all in their appeals for tax relief. The absence of equity in our taxation system caused us Filipino shrimp exporters no small amount of anguish.

During those hard times we were looking up to our government to ensure the survival of our businesses and the jobs of our own people. We did not receive the same privileges given to the multinationals.

Worse, the charge of "dollar salting"

was raised against all shrimp and prawn exporters by the government Task Force on Dollar Salting. Not one exporter was spared this defamation.

Smarting under the whiplash of false rumors and false accusations, we requested for an immediate investigation to clear our names and affirm our good reputation. Sadly, though, with all the voluminous documents submitted, the case was closed without anyone found guilty or declared innocent. Such was the treatment we got from the government mandated by our Constitution to protect us the citizens.

The shrimp and prawn export industry has been a most difficult business as evidenced by the survival of barely a dozen producer-exporters out of more than a hundred processors and exporters who ventured throughout the years.

I can easily say with confidence, however, that the members of SHRIMPEX, despite all obstacles, carried out their export business without committing such alleged wrongdoing as the Task Force on Dollar Salting would have the public believe. Their action only served to dramatize the government's suspicion of private business.

I opposed the arbitrary denunciation of private business as the culprit on dollar salting based on hearsay. Such allegations often result in adverse publicity in media. In turn, such adverse publicity picked up by foreign media affects our foreign buyers to the detriment of our business and, consequently, our country's economy.

In contrast, Taiwan, Thailand,

Indonesia, India, and now even Vietnam are given all the assistance by their governments especially in research and laboratory analyses of soil, water, feed, nutrition, and of fertilizers required in the industry, as well as for their capital requirements to accelerate the pace of development.

The governments of our Asian neighbors have placed

high hopes in the industry as a good foreign exchange earner. In so doing, they have policies that are very supportive of the industry and the entrepreneurs engaged in the business. Their track records show that the industry and the entrepreneurs have not disappointed their governments. The Philippine government should take its cue from them.

I remember a very rewarding visit to Taipei.

I had been there many times but each visit only took me from my hotel to an office building where I would transact business; then I'd fly home as soon as I could without having seen anything much of the place.

Then in 1985, I went to visit the prawn farms in Kaoshiong. It was an entirely different Taipei that I saw; a kinder, warmer, friendlier Taipei. I spent days in the countryside talking to the aquafarmers. I was so fascinated by the strides they have made in the shrimp and prawn industry. I visited their research and laboratory facilities provided by the government.

I was traveling then with George, my COO, who is as serious and totally committed a student as I am. I must have looked funny to our guide, with notebook in hand, continually taking down notes as I observed and studied things they did over there that weren't being done here.

The trip heightened my penchant for writing and doodling. I filled page after page of my notebook with useful information that I was able to use in my book about black tiger prawns. I recommend making such trips.

Business need not be boring and tedious corporate meetings alone. Trips like the one I made to the aquafarms of Taipei can be very relaxing as well as rewarding. It reinforced my self-esteem and helped me overcome some uncertainties I had about the business. It emboldened me to be an example to other entrepreneurs to take business risks and evolve step by step the means to achieve gains and personal success.

The greatest damage
done to the economy however, was the loss of opportunity to develop shrimp production as a great industry.

As early as 1975 we could have provided more employment for our people, earned more foreign exchange, created new ancillary industries, innovated or effected transfer of technology. More importantly, we could have raised the standard of living of rural folks.

Rightly or wrongly, those involved in the shrimp business suspected the government planners of being biased against the aqua farmers. They even started to resent the Marcos government for overlooking the important role of the shrimp and prawn exporters in the national economic program because the government had thrown its full support to businesses such as heavy construction firms like CDCP (now defunct), Disini Group of Companies, and similar huge investments which later proved unfeasible, non-viable, and non-performing.

In January 1988,
the first international conference on shrimps called "SHRIMPS '88 CONFERENCE" was held in Bangkok. There, Dr. Imre Czaves, one of the speakers on prawn development in Asia, congratulated Taiwan for having produced over 50,000 metric tons of shrimps and prawns for that year alone.

Together with the other participants in the conference, I listened in awe and praise of Taiwan's productivity, but I fretted against the easy assumption that, based on such performance, Taiwan was credited with having introduced and promoted the black tiger prawn industry in Japan.

When the moderator asked if there were any questions after the lecture, I lost no time in raising my hand and standing up to correct an erroneous assumption the lecture may have caused.

It wasn't just a matter

of being Filipino. It was also a matter of being honest, a quality that would-be successful entrepreneurs must possess . . . living by principle and being honest in giving credit where credit is due.

So I called attention to the fact that as early as 1976, long before any other country in the world, much less Taiwan, ever conceived of marketing black tiger prawns, our AA Export and Import Corporation exported the first 450 kilograms of black tiger prawns to Japan. This marked the start of our bid to penetrate the Japanese market, an effort which we continued through our network of distributors in Japan.

Our foremost role in the black tiger prawn industry was introducing it to the world market, starting with Japan, as a special prawn specie that would find universal acceptance as a seafood commodity. No one ever dreamed that the lowly black tiger prawn grown accidentally in tandem with milkfish culture would develop into a full-blown commodity and give birth to many ancillary industries in its development, such as:

⊛ Research and Technology on medicines, fertilizers, feeds, vitamins, and nutrients — all essentials to the black tiger prawn growth maintenance.

⊛ Machine, equipment, apparatus — all essentials to the

various stages of prawn growth, from nursing care to grow out sustenance and maintenance, harvesting, processing, and packaging.

I pointed out

that our success created a great impact not only in terms of benefits to the export of the black tiger prawns from the Philippines but also in significant lateral developments in the world scenario of food and agriculture, such as:

⊛ The growth of semi-intensive black tiger prawn monoculture quickly accelerated into super-enterprises.

⊛ Taiwan went first into the industry via the shrimp feed and later to intensive culture.

⊛ Black tiger prawn culture technology spread to other southeast Asian countries like Indonesia and Thailand.

⊛ The black tiger prawn specie was introduced and accepted in the United States and the European Economic Council member countries.

⊛ Ongoing research and development studies in the United States, Taiwan and Japan were intensified and seriously pursued for an improved and higher quality prawn stock and pelletised feed.

With fire

in my voice, I concluded my elucidation on the matter of being first by saying:

"I salute the Filipino people for their natural traits of ingenuity, innovativeness, and unrelenting perseverance which spawned the visualization and creation of the market for the Philippine's black tiger prawns in the world's foremost market — Japan."

From that day on, my co-participants in the conference referred to me as "Prawn Queen of the Philippines." Though done in levity, I took it as a compliment because I have high regard for the amazing prawn that has enhanced my life tremendously.

It is really ironic

and painful that while the Taiwanese used to come to the Philippines to "source" their gravid prawns (for their research and development), they made great strides and earned large revenues through their success in feeds, equipment, and prawns. The Thais came in much later to learn about the industry and today we go to Thailand to learn from them.

We started the marketing, Taiwan developed the pelletized feed and intensive production, then Thailand rode on all available expertise and made a smashing success.

Another major exporter now is Indonesia. Annually, it produces 400,000 metric tons with an export value of US$3 BILLION. Thailand exports 300,000 metric tons and earns US$2.5 BILLION. The Philippines has only 20,000 metric tons valued at around US$250 million. Our AA quality is still the top quality overseas, but our volume is insufficient.

Today, the black tiger prawn is a premium quality commodity in Japan. The United States and Canada have imported sizable volumes of black tiger prawns, yet in many parts of these countries, our prawns have yet to see the shelves of their supermarkets and the dining tables of their residents because the prawns have not yet been introduced to the shopkeepers and the housewives who decide on what to serve their families.

Due to the high cost of advertisement and promotion activities, not enough information about the premium quality of the black tiger prawn reaches consumers. Take, for example, the case of housewives in various parts of the

United States. They are unaware of the existence of this queen of all prawns that is listed high in nutritive value, as well as being very tasty, having juicy meat as well as a delectable cooked smell. Yet it's been two decades already since we introduced this specie to Japan.

Today, many countries are producing this specie under semi-intensive culture. They produce the black tiger prawn that is bluish in color unlike the truly ugly black prawn we started with in 1975.

And so, before we bow out of this business and before government starts to look for other foreign-exchange earning products, let's take stock of our options.

Should we abandon the industry? Oh, NO!

We can't allow that to happen. As early as three years ago I already told our men in government that our shrimp and prawn export can bring in over a billion dollars . . . but no one seems to listen.

If ever there is a product that is readily export-oriented and endowed by God with naturally intrinsic rewards for our people, I dare say it, among others, is the black tiger prawn.

We have a tropical climate that allows the prawn fry to grow strong and healthy throughout the years hence we can grow them in abundance.

We have an abundance of aquaculture coastal land with good waters.

We have an industrious and highly trainable people.

We can produce this product without imported inputs; if at all, these are very minimal.

To whom should I appeal

so our problems and suggested solutions may be addressed properly and acted upon immediately?

So what if Indonesia and Thailand lead the pack? We can match their feat and even surpass it if our government sits up and cooperates. Why, we have the land, we have the business, we have the logistics, but do we have the technology? We need to modernize our methods. We need to do away with our cure approach. It's time to apply the preventive approach using scientific procedures.

Our government can do a lot towards this if they will only give top priority to Philippine shrimp and prawn.

With the stiff competition

in the world market, the Philippine shrimp and prawn export industry needs to take aggressive steps to develop fully.

Our goal for the latter part of the nineties before the decade ends is for the Philippines to regain its supremacy in the industry. We look forward to all-out government support by way of helping the industry:

- maintain excellent quality products;
- improve cost efficiency; and
- increase production.

And how is government

going to accomplish these?

As I have repeated over and over again, our government must recognize the shrimp and prawn to be one of our most important fishery products. The shrimp and prawn export industry is still a sunshine industry. Thailand's export performance of US$2.6 to US$3 billion did not come about from nothing. The Thai exporters had their government's full support and so they did it in just five years time.

We can do better if government would only support us instead of neglecting and, worse, hindering us. That's why I was so encouraged by the positive response of the

Department of Science and Technology (DOST) Secretary William Padolina when I requested his office to jointly and actively work with the private sector to intensify research and development, disseminate information to as many as possible, and establish diagnostic laboratories for better qualitative analysis to serve the aquafarmers.

AA has been in the forefront in this collaboration with government offices like the Department of Agriculture (DA) through the National Agriculture and Fisheries Council (NAFC), the Bureau of Export Trade Promotion (BETP) of DTI, BFAR, and DOST, to assist in giving data on the actual situation of the industry. All of these joint efforts are designed to fully assist all prawn farmers upgrade their technology, increase their production, and make the prawn a strong export product of the Philippines.

We can do it.

We have all the indigenous raw materials available here: vast lands, good waters, skillful manpower. All we need is for the government and the private sector to join hands in mutual cooperation to enhance and make available to all aqua farmers the research and technology they'll need to make a success out of their endeavors. The key is to develop aqua farming technology and continually improve such technology with research.

We need more government executives like Secretary Padolina and Louie Villareal, Executive Director of NAFC. They are the sort of government executives that will lead us to faster economic development. The element of urgency they display is usually missing in government work. It is now time to reverse this attitude of complacency.

For the last eight years (1987-95),

our export production in the shrimp and prawn industry stagnated at US$350 million or less. The projected amount of US$500 million did not materialize because of many firms closing their shrimp and prawn export activities due to:

- World recession;
- Lack of technology to combat the problems of disease;
- Lack of technology to develop better feeds, fertilizers, and vitamins needed by the shrimps and prawns;
- Failure to continually keep abreast with ongoing processes and new inventions;
- Waning enthusiasm among the aqua farmers due to severe losses, making them convert their prawn farms into milkfish farms;
- Confusing land reform policies which made prawn farmers insecure (it was only in late 1995 that the law was passed exempting prawn farmlands from land reform coverage).

All these factors destroyed the momentum of prawn farm development. This caused a drop in hectarage and kept production levels at only US$250 million or less.

We need to reverse this downward trend.

Our dream is to be able to export ONE-BILLION DOLLARS before the next century comes in. When we reach the billion-dollar mark it will be easy to double then triple and quadruple the figure in a few years.

My proposed solutions are:

- Ascertain the hectarage of prawn ponds, their locations, and existing pond conditions.
- Accelerate all the technical knowledge of DOST, DAs and agricultural schools; put up a "FOCUS TEAM" to

work on the problems of production.

• Enhance technology on soil analyses, water balances, feed development, better nutrients, vitamins and fertilizers.

• Increase research on pond diseases and advance knowledge of medicinal approach on these diseases, to the extent of knowing and anticipating new strains of virus P bacteria and being ready with antidotes.

• Allocate funds for research development and dissemination and for maintaining scientific manpower in the organization.

• Disseminate speedily to aqua farmers all necessary information.

• Eliminate burdensome policies on taxation as well as fees that hinder progress of the industry and render it uncompetitive in the global market.

• Give full priority to marketing and promoting the industry.

If government sets the pace
and joins the private sector in upgrading our prawn export industry, success is assured.

As for transferring the technology to the aqua farmers, we can start with a laboratory. Provide all adequate research and lab testing facilities accessible to the shrimp and prawn farmer. There is no substitute for knowledge, experience, skill and all the information they can get to make a success of the business. It will not cost the government much to make existing research centers responsive to the needs of aqua farmers in strategic points in the country. With enough government support, we can reach the BILLION-DOLLAR MARK BEFORE YEAR 2000.

We can all ride the tiger to success again!

Chapter Four

<u>Kia Pride: The People's Car</u>

DAVID
AND
GOLIATHS

To pioneer

is to choose a lonely and frightful road to walk. But to fight against a giant cartel? You not only go the lonely and frightful road, but you take a thorny, rocky, and doubly lonely and frightful road full of pitfalls for the unwary and weak of heart.

But I decided to pioneer and to fight a giant cartel, not for personal motivations of profit, but to change the status quo. A status quo that was so disadvantageous and discriminatory against the countless, faceless, middle-class working Filipinos who were then denied their right to have access to an affordable — yet high-quality — people's car.

Cars were initially imported

from various overseas sources as completely built-up (CBU) units until 1950, when controls were imposed and importers had to establish plants to assemble completely knocked-down units.

1972 saw the rationalization of the industry with the launching of the Progressive Car Manufacturing Program (PCMP) wherein the 19 previous assemblers were reduced to a maximum of five (5) participants.

From a mere 747 units in 1953, sales grew to a peak of 14,227 in 1979 before the full effects of the oil crisis brought down the demand to 11,994 by 1982. Sales deteriorated further during the crisis years to 6,355 units in 1984 and bottomed at 3,460 in 1986.

With the improvement in the economy, sales grew and jumped by 60% to 5,543 in 1987 and soared further by 99.1% to 11,038 units in 1988 sales.

The five (5) original participants of PCMP

were Canlubang Automotive Resources Corporation (Mitsubishi), Delta Motor Corporation (Toyota), D.M.G. Inc. (Volkswagen), Ford Philippines, Inc. (Ford); and General Motors Pilipinas, Inc. (GM/Opel/Isuzu). In 1982, Pilipinas Nissan, Inc. (Nissan), acquired the manufacturing facilities and program participation of D.M.G., Inc..

Even though only five participants were allowed by the program, other brand makers were able to participate because it appeared that then President Ferdinand Marcos gave special concessionary permits to makers of Mercedes Benz, Renault, and Chrysler.

With the downturn of the economy, however, the car manufacturers left one at a time. First to go was Delta Motor Corporation when the Development Bank of the Philippines foreclosed its assets in 1984. Ford Philippines, Inc., which had brought a stamping plant over to Mariveles, Bataan, announced its withdrawal from the country that same year and completely ceased operations in 1985. It sold its stamping plant to China. D.M.G., which gave us the first people's car, the Volkswagen "Beetle" which had been an overnight success because it catered to the needs of every level of our society, also had to close shop. The last to leave was General Motors Pilipinas, Inc.. It left in 1986.

The Yulos who were the majority owners of Canlubang Automotive Resources Corporation which eventually became PAMCOR sold out too. In Yulo's case, the BOI, in violation of our laws, allowed the sale of their shares to their Japanese partners, thus making PAMCOR a 100% Japanese owned company.

As a result of the February

22-26, 1986, military coup, Mrs. Corazon Aquino was installed the new President of the Philippines.

Her government discarded the Progressive Car Manufacturing Program of Marcos. In its place, Memorandum Order No. 136 dated December 1, 1987, promulgated the Car Development Program (CDP) with mainly the same objectives as its predecessor. The only difference was that while the PCMP allowed five participants (with additional ones on a case-to-case basis), the CDP limited the participants to three.

The PCMP had participants making various brands such as Ford, Chrysler, GM from US, Mitsubishi, Isuzu from Japan, and Toyota. In contrast, the CDP of Aquino limited the brands to three, all Japanese, namely Mitsubishi, Toyota, and Nissan.

The participants and their shareholders were:
1. PHILIPPINE AUTOMOTIVE CORP. (PAMCOR)
   Mitsubishi Motor Corp. (Japanese)
   Nissho Iwai Corp. (Japanese)
2. PILIPINAS NISSAN, INC. (PNI)
   Marubeni Corp. (Japanese)

Nissan Motor Co. Ltd. (Japanese)
Mantrasco Group (Filipino)
3. TOYOTA MOTOR PHILIPPINES CORP. (TMPC)
Toyota Motor Corp. (Japanese)
Mitsui & Co. Ltd. (Japanese)
MetroBank/George Ty Group (Filipino)

The BOI intended the CDP

to be its vehicle in promoting and developing the domestic car industry. The rub was in their limiting the participants to only three — and these were exclusively Japanese manufacturers. The firms were controlled and managed by Japanese shareholders.

The CDP objectives were:
- Development of a viable automotive parts manufacturing industry;
- Technology transfer and development;
- Employment generation;
- Reasonable consumer prices of passenger cars; and
- Foreign exchange savings and earnings.

The Department of Trade and Industry (DTI) through the BOI, was the agency responsible for carrying out the effective implementation of the Program.

The terms of the program

were defined thus:
- Passenger Car — shall refer to a motor vehicle that is used primarily for the transport of persons, including passenger car derivative vans not covered by any other vehicle development program.
- Local Parts — are defined as those locally manufactured parts and components that are of OEM approved quality, of reasonable price, and of a maximum cost penalty of 15%.

Cost penalty shall mean the percentage by which the selling price of a locally produced part is greater than the landed cost of its imported counterpart.

⊛ Local Content Rate of Parts — the percentage of net local content over selling price or manufacturing cost if the parts are produced in-house. Net local content corresponds to the OEM selling price of imported raw materials, components and supplies used in the production of the product.

⊛ CKD — (completely-knocked-down) parts and components for assembly purposes that are imported in disassembled condition. The CKD pack, however, may include not only parts and components, but also sub-assemblies and assemblies, e.g., engine, transmission, axle assemblies. The bodies and chassis must be imported in completely disassembled condition and must be assembled and painted locally.

⊛ SKD — (semi-knocked-down) parts/components for assembly purposes that are imported in partially assembled condition. SKDs include semi-assembled vehicles.

⊛ CBU — (completely-built-up) vehicles imported in completely assembled form and ready for use by the consumers.

CDP covered the manufacturing

and assembly of passenger cars up to 2,800 cc. engine displacement. All passenger cars covered in the program were to be imported in CKD condition only. Only the qualified participants under the program were allowed to manufacture and assemble passenger cars. The importation of new and second-hand completely-built-up (CBU) cars covered by the CDP was not allowed except for the following:

⊛ Those passenger cars covered under Central Bank

circulars governing no-dollar imports and motor vehicles by diplomatic officials.

⊛ Those passenger cars imported by participants prototype units for evaluation purposes limited to two (2) units for each model variant.

⊛ Those passenger cars with engine displacement of 2,500 cc. to 2,800 cc. imported by BOI-registered tourist-oriented service enterprises not later than July 31, 1988, with prior approval of the President and in accordance with the guidelines for such importations agreed between the Department of Tourism (DOT) and the BOI, subject to the approval of the President.

By the time the CDP was set up,

there was already an accelerating demand for cars for the working Filipino especially those in the middle-income bracket. A demand-supply gap ensued, causing the manufacturers to incur extensive delivery lags.

Let me mention briefly that when the Aquino government replaced that of Marcos in 1986, Toyota was given the privilege to buy the dead asset of the government's part of the foreclosed Delta Motor Corporation of Ricardo Silverio. The government allegedly sold 1/3 of the facilities to Toyota for over a million pesos.

With their purchase, Toyota was immediately given the third slot in the car program, with help from MetroBank. In 1987-1989, they were given the exclusive right to service the entire automotive needs of the country, together with two other firms, as the chosen participants in Aquino's car program.

One must keep in mind that the country had long been in drought; there was no manufacturing nor importation of new cars. The people were using old cars, 10 to 20 years old, kept running only by constant repairs and maintenance. But neither Toyota nor the other two members of the program could cope with the rising demand for new cars.

For a year, Toyota was allowed to bring in knocked-down cars (cars without tires or batteries). Just the same, this did not favorably solve the problem of providing the working class with affordable cars. Consumers had to wait for months on end to get their units inspite of sizeable downpayments. Some even resorted to adding as much as P30,000 to P50,000 to their downpayments just to be given priority in the delivery of their units. The cartelized structure of the CDP left the people no choice but to wait at the convenience of the participants of the program.

The prices of brand-new cars

produced by the participants were constantly rising and attained levels beyond the reach of most Filipinos, including those in the middle-income brackets.

The lowest-priced model in the market was PNI'S Nissan Sentra 1300 LX which retailed at P252,000.00, followed by TMPC's Toyota Corolla 1300 XL at P276,000.00 and PAMCOR'S Mitsubishi Lancer 1300 EL at P280,000.00. The high prices of these models were due to two key factors:
• Dependence on a single strong currency. Since all of the imported components required by the limited participants were exclusively sourced from Japan or its affiliates, manufacturing costs were subject to the appreciation movement of the strong Japanese yen. From 1980 to 1988, the Philippine peso had depreciated on cross rates against the yen 5.3 times, thereby geometrically inflating car prices in peso terms.
• Lack of "People's Car" models. While other countries

enjoy the availability of lower-cost cars, the CDP participants refrained from making these lower-margin models.
The lowest engine displacements produced for the domestic
markets were of 1300 c.c. configurations. These were larger
and more expensive than the 1000 and 1100 c.c. models
envisioned by BOI as affordable "people's cars."

The anomalous situation

caused by the shortage of having to queue and pay
additional amounts to dealers just to be allotted a car,
spawned a form of corruption wherein enterprising
businessmen brought in cars through the so-called "chop-
chop" process.

This "chop-chop" process means the cutting into
half of cars and bringing them into the country as car
parts. As such, the duties and taxes on them were
drastically reduced. The car halves are then welded
together and sold as CBU units. Because of the crisis
in demand and supply, even more enterprising people
brought in cars in containers and declared these as
things other than cars.

It is when cars are priced high and imports are
prohibitive that some ingenious traders will bring in
these cars through various methods, either through
parallel imports of CBU units or "chop-chop" parts.

To my mind, the whole mess was due to a poorly
conceived car program. If the PMCP was a failure,
then the CDP which was nothing more than a poor
imitation of the first program was equally weak.
Nothing innovative but simply full of regulations. It
was even conceived to be anti-Filipino (as the three
participants were all Japanese) and anti-consumer (as
the cars were all pegged to a single currency, the

Japanese yen, which at one time continued to appreciate and thus shackled us to a high-priced currency).

The element of competition was totally eliminated by this BOI policy. There was no price war because the three car makers were friendly and cooperative with one another. Their price ranges were almost identical, with very minor variations. There was a booming car demand and for the duration of the three years exclusivity, only the three Japanese firms enjoyed the privilege. Thanks to the government's myopic policy.

It was under this climate of ineffectual
car programming that my partner and I participated in a bidding to buy the old facilities of the Delta II plant. Toyota had bought 1/3 and the goverment was auctioning off the remaining 2/3 of their non-performing asset. Our firm, Columbian Motors Corporation (CMC), bought half of the 2/3 remaining property at P215 million, which was about P73 million more than that offered by the next highest bidder.

Our original intention in buying the property was to buy it as an investment and resell it later as real estate. The anomalous situation, however, caused by the inept program challenged me to look for solutions and, considering that at least 70% of the plant would remain unused for Columbian Motor's immediate purposes, I challenged my partner to embark with me on a people's car program that would maximize the use of the plant as well as solve the problem of supply lag.

My partner felt that it would be difficult to upstage the program. I reasoned out, however, that since programs are made by people and people do make mistakes, the technocrats who made the program had made a big mistake. Their program failed to meet the people's needs. In fact, it only served the interests of the three Japanese makers. Therefore, I told my partner, we had to fight the defective program by coming up with a people's car program of our own.

One does not just go and tell the President

that there's something wrong with the government's program unless one can come up with a better one. The wise entrepreneur must first arm himself with facts and alternatives.

We scouted around for a car that our average Filipino citizen could afford. We found it in Korea. It was a car made by KIA Motors Co., called the KIA Pride. It was less than 1200 c.c., with a very high performance in Korea. It was a car sold not just in Korea but also in the United States under Ford, as FESTIVA, as well as in Taiwan. The KIA Motor Corporation is an alliance of KIA of Korea, MAZDA of Japan, and FORD of U.S.A. We had found our David of a car with which to fight the giant car cartel.

We lost no time in writing to the BOI

about our intentions. We cited the following reasons to bolster our argument that the car program be opened to us:
⊛ We have bought a non-performing asset of the government for P215 million.
⊛ The property has facilities and equipment to make cars and it would be such a waste not to use them.
⊛ We intend to make the People's Car which is not available in the market and that it will be sold at P175,000.00 if allowed under the foreign exchange rate of P22.00 to US$1.00, and it will be consistently available at all times.

We envisioned the People's Car Program

to gain the interest if not the immediate approval of the
BOI because it would:

• Not only offer affordable cars to the average Filipino
family but would also help replenish the fast-vanishing
fleet of Metro Manila taxis;

• Provide competition against the existing car manufacturers
and succeed in lowering the prices to more reasonable
levels; and

• Eventually break up the seemingly invincible Japanese
cartel since CMC, unlike the existing car participants, is not
constrained from sourcing from countries other than Japan.

The DTI/BOI advised us to give the CDP participants
adequate time to prove themselves and rectify the situation.
So we waited for signs of improvement in the industry.
Unfortunately, there was none. Thus, on July 3, 1989, we
(thru CMC) sent a letter to the Trade Secretary formally
submitting and outlining our proposal. Stony silence was the
only reply we received.

I understood that the BOI did not

want to change their three-member program because they
had promised the Japanese car makers that there would be
only the three of them on the rationale that when there were
five, the program failed. The BOI believed that three was a
viable number. It did not matter to them, so it seemed, that
the cars being made were not priced within the reach of the
average consumer.

The three participants also refrained from making the
lower-cost model cars with engine displacements of 1000 to
1200 cc as envisioned by the BOI as affordable people's car;
instead, they produced big car models that justified their
prohibitive prices.

It was so unfair to the Filipino
consumer . . . the maneuverings of the three program
participants to serve their interests without serving the
needs of the people whose government had given them
the privilege to do business in the country.

I further countered the BOI claim that three
participants to the program was viable by pointing out
that they had denied our people the right to a freer choice
by binding us to one currency source for our automotive
industry. As early as then, I warned that the yen will
grow even stronger against our peso and that we will be
faced with the spectre of buying more and more expensive
cars in the future unless something was done about it
fast. I even prophesied in a public hearing that the day
will come when the yen will appreciate to a hundred yen
or below to the US dollar. No one believed me. The yen
seemed invincible.

I questioned why the industry should be left in the
hands of three Japanese firms which practically dominated
the car industry Why can't the Filipinos be part of the
program? Not just as shareholders, but as active managers
and makers. I kept up with this kind of argument to the
BOI, which kept countering that the three Japanese
participants were enough.

Sometime in 1988, President
Cory Aquino made her first trip to Europe for the purpose of
building diplomatic relations and selling the Philippines to
Europe for bilateral trade and investment.

With her were some businessmen. I was invited to
join them so I could sell my black tiger prawns to Europe
too. At that time, the black tiger prawn was having difficulty
in the market due to a lull in the market in Japan. The

Japanese Emperor was taken ill and the people of Japan, in deference to him, avoided eating exotic foods. Hence the decrease in demand for Philippine shrimps and prawns.

So I joined President Aquino's mission for two reasons:
- To sell my black tiger prawns to Europe.
- To have the opportunity to talk to the President and give her a copy of my project study on why I should be allowed to make the people's car.

Sure enough, while on the plane above the Pacific Ocean crossing to Europe, I was able to talk to her about my desire to build the people's car. Her comment after I had explained to her the whys and wherefores was: "Elena, if you can really sell it cheap, go ahead."

I was so happy with her remark. To me, it was an encouragement and an affirmation that I was right about wanting to build a people's car. Buoyed by the President's encouraging comment, I immediately looked for the Trade Secretary and asked him to go with me to see President Aquino so he could hear for himself how she approved of my plan, but he said: "No, Elena, the President doesn't know about the car program. Let us not bother her."

My boldness in leaving my business class accommodation in the plane to go to the first class accomodation where President Cory Aquino was seated with her cabinet came to no avail.

The Secretary of Trade was adamant in keeping the participants in the car program to his so-called viable number: Three. He told me so right in front of Oscar Hilado and Ramon del Rosario. He kept stressing that we must go with the program. I was shocked to hear that the President herself had no inkling about the unviable program that was a monopoly of Japanese-owned firms. A veritable car cartel. I had to leave it at that for that moment. Ramon del Rosario even commented: *"Sorry ka na lang,* Elena." ("Tough luck for you, Elena.")

True, I made no headway with the BOI,

but on that European trip, I made the aquaintance of a businessman, Mr. Roger Vandenberghe, who approached me in Belgium and offered the distributorship of a good European truck under the brand name of DAF. When he first approached me in my Philippine booth, I asked him pointblank, "You want some prawns?" because that was what I was selling in my exhibition booth.

"No! I want to give you my DAF trucks. I want you to assemble them because these are far more superior than all the Japanese trucks combined. You can sell them at a competitive price with better quality, too."

Well, that was one interesting development during that trip. But the most important was President Aquino's favorable comment which really buoyed me up. On our return from Europe, I pursued my case even more ardently. I wrote a follow-up letter to the BOI for them to open up the program to other manufacturers, specifically to me and my partners.

My position was that our firm

would have the capability and efficiency to produce both commercial vehicles and passenger cars for the local market, owing to our ownership of the M.A.N. Division Plant of the defunct Delta Motor Corp. which is equipped with advanced vehicle manufacturing facilities.

I also cited that the expected combined production of the three program participants would reach only 33,000 for the year against the projected demand of 40,000 units.

I also reiterated that our firm proposed to initially

introduce affordable "people's car" models with engine displacements below 1200 cc principally sourced from South Korea whose currency has not been as strong as the Japanese yen. The units were to start on SKD basis for immediate availability in the domestic markets. It was further stressed that our firm, CMC, had the capability to produce 12,000 cars annually on a single shift, and assemble CKD packs shortly after. The foreign exchange credits required for importations would be programmed to be repaid from the export credits of a three-year $64.8M CBU export program for 4x4 off-road commercial vehicles.

Aside from my letter to the Secretary of Trade, I also wrote a letter to President Cory Aquino. I firmly believed that she would respond to my letter in a positive way that would prod the Secretary of Trade to allow us to join the CDP, such that I sent my letter written in my own handwriting.

Unfortunately, the President trusted her Trade Secretary to make all the trade policy decisions and so, she forwarded all communications, including my letter to her, to the Secretary of Trade. I believe that the Secretary, being averse to my idea that there should be more than three participants in the program, did not find it meritorious to act on my proposal. But because I refused to give up and kept on following up with the BOI, they finally reconsidered their decision. Tenacity is truly part of entrepreneurship.

My continuous follow-up letters

somehow found support in the private sector.

The Rotary Club invitations became a platform for me to speak out my mind. I talked to a number of these clubs even as far as Roxas City. My thrust was always the same: Demand for a people's car. I was just a simple businesswoman trying to do my thing, but the objections I had to hurdle honed my speaking prowess.

I always asked my audience to support me by taking a stand on the matter. Many did. They expressed moral support by conveying their opinions to me, to their friends, both in government and private offices. Others wrote to the media and Congress, and even to DTI. People after all found me sensible and my cause worth supporting.

A year passed before a public hearing was called by BOI. Many interested parties and persons came to the hearing. Represented were the consumer groups, taxi operators, parts makers, and interested participants.

The hearing was opened by Undersecretary Lilia Bautista. She asked me to start the discussion.

"Madam Chairman, thank you," I said, "for your willingness to hear our side. Let me start by saying that this present program has to be revised because it is not doing our economy good. It is a program that is biased against the Filipino. It is a program that does not induce growth of our economy.

"One of the basic needs of our working class is a car — for mobility. Already, we are having strikes because there is not enough supply to meet the demands of the people. Our public transport is inadequate. What is needed is a small car that can easily fit the average family's budget.

"If there are three or more working members in a family, they can easily pool their financial resources to buy the model car I have in mind. As it is, no matter how they try to combine resources, they will never be able to afford the cars made by these Japanese car makers which range from 400,000 pesos up. The car I am suggesting will only cost about 175,000 pesos at the rate of 22 pesos to one dollar in the foreign exchange."

"Besides," I hastened to stress, "isn't it said that it is not good to put all our goods in one basket? How come we have a situation here where all the participants in the program are all Japanese? That is binding us to a strong currency, the yen. Time will come when their money will be so powerful owing to Japan's strong economy that the rate of exchange will reach a 100 yen or even less."

At the time I said that, what I predicted was unthinkable. But time has proved me right. The rate of exchange has reached as low as 89 yen to a dollar. In hindsight, had the BOI listened to me then, the People's Car would have benefited many consumers earlier and not much, much later.

"I am not invading their high-priced market," I reassured her, "but I am just thinking of those who only need a decent car to go to school with . . . and how about those who must get to the office on time? A people's car will fit their needs and their modest income. Why, in Europe," I stressed, "they use small cars over there to economize on gas. We Filipinos can do the same.

"Lastly," I continued, "no industry should be closed to Filipinos. I am not against the multinationals, but I deplore this situation that allows them to participate in an industry that is closed to the Filipino. No industry should be closed to the Filipino in his own country.

"Why," I concluded, "can I go to Japan and do something there that the Japanese won't allow me to? We are in our own country. The Filipino should be allowed to determine the direction of his own economy . . . we have the right to do so. All efforts must be made to make the Filipino an active economic participant in any area he can capably contribute . . ."

I know I must have said a mouthful but those were the principal points I wanted to impress on the BOI. And as I was talking, I noticed the absence of the three Japanese participants. Only Henry Moran, their spokesman was there, and I took the opportunity to point this out.

"Isn't it that there are three Japanese brand car makers? How come they speak through one mouthpiece . . . Henry Moran? Isn't this clear proof that there exists a Cartel? Japan Incorporated is at work," I said. In truth, I never saw at any of our hearings, congressional or otherwise, the Japanese owner or executive of any of the three participants in the car program. It seemed they all had one mind, one voice, and one mouthpiece . . . Mr. Henry Moran, their spokesman.

After I had concluded, a guy stood up to say that he was a taxi operator, but that his taxis were already old and dilapidated and he didn't know how he could replace them because he was required to "line up" to request for replacements but that the queue was rather long and the waiting period seemed endless. Other listeners in the hearing gave their own commendation for a people's car and aired their complaints against the unaffordability of the cars under the program. There was no one who favored maintaining the status quo, but it was clear by the end of the hearing that the people were clamoring for their kind of car.

The BOI's attitude,

however, was: "We shall see the trend . . ." The media, however, did not remain silent. I had succeeded in making a lot of noise. There were those who looked favorably on my plans, and there were a few who derided me and made fun of our capability to engage in the industry since we had "no experience except in the electronic industry."

All the hullaballoo concerning the program prompted another hearing. This time, in Congress. There, in the hallowed halls of Congress, together with my partner

Mr. Jose Alvarez, Jr., we explained to the investigating parties why we considered the program unfair. We also projected for them the growth of the car industry and presented to them the same arguments we gave at the BOI hearing. But despite the Congressional hearing, the favorable resolution that would have given us the right to join the car program still did not materialize quickly.

The opposition seemed formidable.

To my mind, there was only one thing to be done. I had to present my case before the very people I was fighting for. I had to sacrifice my privacy. I allowed myself to be interviewed. Though I'm a very private person, trying to keep a low profile, I had to come out of my hibernation.

I'm sure that in those days, I must have seemed obnoxious to the BOI. I encouraged the public to articulate their desire for affordable, small model cars. I didn't mind being made fun of by some columnists who were unsympathetic to our cause. All I wanted to do was to use all possible avenues opened to me in fighting the cartel. For breaking up the cartel would be a breakthrough for KIA PRIDE, the People's Car.

I was determined to win the fight for the right of the Filipino . . . the working class, the junior executives, the parents who need to take their children to school before going on to their jobs . . . they have the right to be mobile, to have their own cars. For them, I had to be strong. I brought the case before them, and they responded positively.

The BOI conducted another hearing

on October 18, 1989. Finally, the program was opened! It

was opened to everybody, but the guidelines were rather onerous.

In the public hearing conducted that October 18, 1989, the BOI disclosed that it was considering the opening of a new car category for models with engine displacements of 1100 c.c. and below, subject to the following conditions:
- Price freeze for three years;
- Minimum of of 51% local content;
- Local manufacture of major components; and
- 50% export credit shall be for 100% automotive related exports, among others.

According to the BOI, the primary objective of this proposal was to address the need for more affordable cars to benefit a larger car segment of the population.

Adverse reaction
to the BOI's proposed guidelines were many:
- While the current CDP participants which catered to a smaller privileged sector could raise their prices, the interested producers of "People's Cars" would have difficulty in ensuring even near-term viability with an unrealistic and arbitrary price freeze condition over a medium term.
- Although the present participants have the vast financial and technological resources to achieve 51% local content, they are required to only attain 36% in 1989 and 40% in 1990.
- Current participants were allowed to earn foreign exchange credits through exports of non-automotive related products while exports of makers of the "People's Cars" must be 100% automotive related.

It appeared that in its eagerness to attract foreign investors, the BOI created an industrial base dominated by overseas giants at the expense of struggling but dedicated

Filipino entrepreneurs who only sought to succeed with an equal chance to do business in their own country.

On December 16, 1989,

BOI press releases indicated a little softening of its heart:
- The new category was 1200 c.c. and below;
- The price ceiling was set at P175,000 retail price inclusive of tax, but with an adjustment clause to cover movements in taxes, wages, foreign exchange rates and CKD components;
- Export credits of non-automotive related products would be allowed; and
- 51% local content must be achieved by 1992.

It was unfortunate that no official guidelines covering the new category had been released by the BOI, except for releases to the press which are not binding nor official; thus making the Filipino car buyer wait longer.

We were sent a notice

to file our application following certain requirements, with the explicit instruction to fulfill these requirements within a very short time! Such rules were never imposed on TOYOTA who, upon investing in 1/3 of the government non-performing asset which was part of the defunct DELTA MOTOR CORP., was immediately given the third slot in the CDP. CMC, our firm, on the other hand, was given designed-to-discourage guidelines which we followed nonetheless. We toed the line, so to speak.

It took a long time for BOI to adjudicate due to the large number of applicants.

They eventually approved more than five. Isn't it puzzling if not amusing to recall that when I first applied for the program, the DTI and the BOI would not approve because, according to them, the program would be rendered unviable were the number of participants to exceed three.

Now that they had decided to approve the making of the people's car, they could not be satisfied with less than five; the number they had found unviable at the start. I have long given up trying to find logic in government thinking.

By the time they approved of our proposal to manufacture the people's car, the peso had already been devalued to the rate of almost P30.00 to one US dollar or, at best, at P28.50 to a dollar. So, the cost of the KIA Pride per unit rose to P225,000.00 instead of our promised P175,000.00.

People could hardly understand when we told them that the price had not changed at all as promised by the KIA firm in Korea. It was still the same when expressed in the US dollar currency. The jacked-up price was due to the peso devaluation . . . from P22.00 to P28.50 per US dollar, thus increasing the original price of P175,000.00 to P225,000.00 per unit. Still, it was cheaper than any of the over P400,000.00 per unit cost of the Japanese brand cars.

After the KIA Pride

had been in the market for some time, a friend disclosed to me that he had bought a car, but not a KIA, for P50,000.00 less than the original standard price. I told him that I didn't mind his not buying KIA Pride . . . in fact, I was happy that, because of me, he got a car at lower cost. Because of competition, the big-three manufacturers dropped their prices by P50,000.00, a thing unheard of in their history. Had it not been for the KIA Pride, the People's Car, the prices of the cars made by the Car Cartel would have risen steadily. We had succeded in bringing the people's car to the people. We had won our case. It brought a good competition that offered a choice to the consumers. Because of this, the prices of Japanese cars came down.

Yes, we won our cause, and although

those other applicants who had been approved with us had not immediately joined the program, it did not matter to us.

Normally, BOI gives time constraints for submitting schedules for compliance of their approval requirements. In our case, we were given only about three months to comply, which we did. Failure to comply would mean non-approval. That no time constraints were given to the other applicants is not a matter of complaint.

I am happy to note that there are others who would join the program. This will bring a healthy environment for business competition that will redound to consumers' benefit. But I did complain of a case when a participant broke the people's car pricing rule by selling their cars over and above the approved P225,000/unit by adding additional receipts of so-called accessories amounting to over P100,000.00. In effect, said car was marketed at P325,000.00 and not P225,000.00.

If at all, the complaint was simply to correct the situation and not to cause injury to anyone. As a matter of fact, when personally approached by the executive of the people's car participant, I told him I truly welcomed their entry into the industry and that I believe that their cars are quality cars and should approximately belong to the higher end models.

Since their entry was only possible through the people's car program, they were even suffering losses at the prices they were selling. At any rate, I told him that by not pursuing my complaint with the BOI, I was already helping them. I assured him of my cooperation and wished his company well in its business. Today, this car participant is No. 1 or 2 in the automotive industry.

All these difficulties

that the DTI, the BOI, and our competitors threw our way were clear signs of their desire to keep the CDP "Magic 3" intact. But to no avail. All these difficulties only served to sweeten our victory. We made it. KIA Pride made it. The giant that was the Car Cartel was finally broken up and the People's Car broke through. The real winner? The real beneficiary? Not us. No less than the indomitable Filipinos . . . the average Filipino citizens who now, finally, have their People's Car.

To me, it matters not that today, we are not the top seller of cars in the Philippines. Being on top is not the point. We always try our best and that's what counts. But having dismantled the cartel, the choice is wide. Had I not fought this battle in 1989, perhaps, the story would be different today.

I know for sure that once a cartel is entrenched solidly, it's hard to unravel. Further, it would be almost impossible to put up late structures to catch up with fully entrenched developed capabilities.

My joy is full. There is freedom of choice. There is good for the greatest number of people.

The Lim family. Joseph and Elena with children (from left) Susan, David, son-in-law George Tan, Jason, and Vincent.

The Solid family. Joseph and Elena Lim pose with some of Solid's top executives.

Elena S. Lim (ESL) posing with Nobuo Kanoi and other executives of Sony Corporation and Solid Corporation. Seated from left to right: Sony representative to the Philippines Takayoshi Hirota, Tsotumo Murata (Sony), Chairman Joseph Lim (Solid), Deputy President Nobuo Kanoi (Sony), ESL, Solid Corporation EVP Susan L. Tan, Kenji Tamiya and Takao Yuhara (Sony). Standing behind them are other Sony and Solid executives.

DTI Secretary Jose S. Concepcion with ESL, Undersecretary Raul Boncan, Marivic Concepcion and Maribel Ongpin (extreme left).

DTI Secretary Jose Concepcion with Mr. Nobuo Kanoi, Deputy President of Sony Corporation, Japan, touring plant facilities during the inauguration of Solid Corporation's manufacturing facilities in Valenzuela, MM in September 1989.

Nobuo Kanoi, Deputy President of SONY Corporation, assisted by Kenji Tamiya, planting the inaugural tree during the inauguration of new facilities in Bulacan for audio/video products.

Plaque commemorating the establishment of new production facilities in Bulacan.

Kenji Tamiya, Nobuo Kanoi, Joseph Lim, and ESL pose for posterity beside the commemorative plaque of Inaugural Tree at Solid's Bulacan factory.

The shrimp processing plant in Tacloban City.

The shrimp processing plant of AA Export and Import Corporation in Tacloban City.

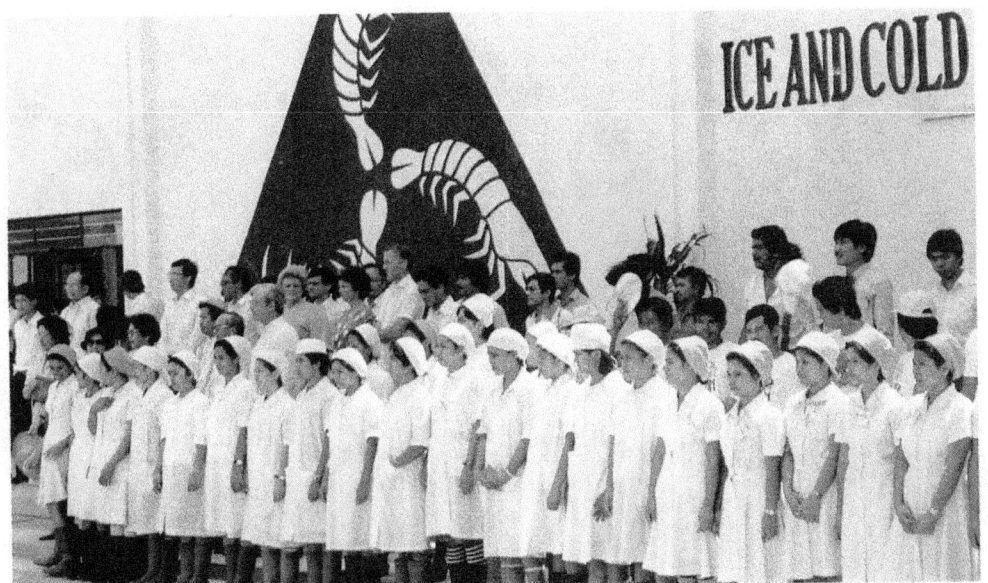

Part of the labor complement at the prawn processing plant in Bacolod City.

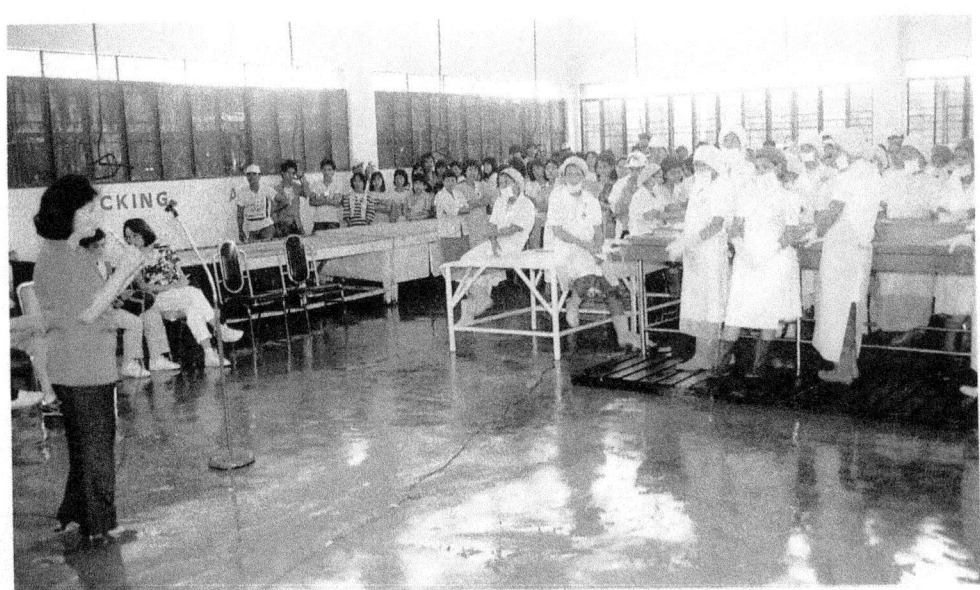

ESL before workers in the Bacolod City plant, expounding on the future and potentials of the prawn industry.

Customs Commissioner and former AFP Vice Chief of Staff Lt. Gen. Salvador Mison with wife Ione (extreme left) and ESL observe lobster processing at Tacloban, Leyte plant.

Workers in the prawn processing plant sorting export-quality prawns.

DTI Deputy Minister Edgardo Tordesillas (2nd from right) inspecting frozen blocks of prawns at the Roxas plant. At right is George Tan, EVP and COO of the aquaculture business.

Ambassador Reginald Dorrett of Canada welcomed at airport on way to visit Bacolod City prawn processing plant. Also shown are Bill and Margarette Gooch of the Canadian embassy.

ESL at the San Juanico bridge with Trade and Industry Deputy Minister and concurrent BOI Managing Head Edgardo Tordesillas. Also shown are Marinela Fabella, Josie Tordesillas and Margarette Gooch.

ESL with son David enjoying a light moment at San Juanico bridge. Behind them is the beautiful island of Samar.

Visitors and guests touring the prawn hatchery and grow-out operations pond at the Roxas City plant.

Technician showing Bill Gooch of the Canadian embassy the growth stages of prawn fries.

George R. Tan, EVP and COO of aquaculture operations addressing employees during annual HRD seminar.

ESL in one of the Congressional Committee hearings leading to the revision of the government's Car Development Program (CDP). The expanded CDP eventually allowed more participants and introduction of the "People's Car" model, the Kia Pride.

ESL in Korea, with executives of Kia Motors Corporation. Car model shown is the Kia Pride, which was successfully introduced to the Philippine market in 1990. L-R: Jose Ch. Alvarez, Jr., Gus Abaya, ESL, Yung Gul Yoo, President of Kia Service Corp., and Ick Ho Um, Chairman, Korphil Corp..

A Kia Pride rolling off the assembly line. Each unit is subjected to strict manufacturing and quality inspection standards. Thousands of satisfied Kia Pride owners have enjoyed the comfort and affordability that this truly people's car has offered.

The Administration Building of Laguna International Industrial Park (LIIP), a 117-hectare industrial park in Ganado and Mamplasan, Biñan, Laguna; a joint-venture project with Samsung Corporation

Solid Corporation Chairman Joseph Lim and LIIP Chairperson ESL greet Ambasador Chang-Soo Lee of South Korea during the dual ceremonies inaugurating LIIP and the new Biñan Interchange.

Among the dignitiaries who spoke during the inauguration of LIIP were Senate President Edgardo Angara and Speaker Jose de Venecia, 2nd and 4th from left, respectively. Also shown are David S. Lim, S.W. Lee, President of Samsung Fine Chemical Co., Ltd., C.M. Rhee, EVP of Citizen's National Bank of Korea, and Director Yong Ho Oh of Samsung Corp..

VIPs and guests led by Trade and Industry Secretary Rizalino S. Navarro (in Barong Tagalog, with lei) during the inauguration of LIIP's Administration Building.

Shown at the ribbon during the inauguration of LIIP. From left to right: Presidential Adviser Hilarion Henares, C.M. Rhee, Y.H. Oh, Samsung Co., Ltd. EVP S. W. Lee, David S. Lim ESL, Korean Ambassador C. S. Lee, DTI Secretary Rizalino S. Navarro, EPZA Deputy Administrator E. Vigo, Mr. Kim, and Laguna Governor Restituto Luna.

New Biñan Interchange turnover. ESL turns over to DTI Secretary R.S. Navarro letter of donation and commemorative plaque symbolizing cooperation between the private sector and government.

ESL and DTI Secretary R.S. Navarro planting the inaugural LIIP tree. At back is Angel Ornedo, LIIP General Manager.

Shown is a portion of the P140 million Biñan Interchange (donated by LIIP to the Philippine government) cutting across South Expressway.

The Laguna International Industrial Park.

The Management Association of the Philippines (MAP) is the most prestigious organization of top executives in the Philippines. As a governor of the MAP board and chairperson of its Agribusiness and Countryside Development Committee, ESL meets weekly with her colleagues. Here she shares a light moment with them. Left to right: Larry Henares, Phil Juntereal, ESL, Ace Fernandez, Al Guerzon, Joe Madamba, and Manny Lim, Jr..

God, what do we do? This construction worker seems to be scouring the heavens for an answer . . . Photo taken before the start of construction work on the Kita factory at the lahar-devastated Clark field in Pampanga.

The stark desolation wrought by lahar from Mt. Pinatubo that greeted ESL during her first visit to the Kita site. The long wall in the background had to be levelled prior to construction of the Kita factory. It blistered many hands and broke down many tools before finally giving in.

A day of jubilation and fulfillment. A phoenix rises out of the ashes. Ribbon-cutting ceremonies during the Kita inauguration, November 24, 1995. Left to right: Joseph Lim, Dr. Susumo Yoshida, Senate President Edgardo Angara, ESL, and Victor Lim, Chairman of the Bases Conversion Development Authority (BCDA).

A testament to the indomitable Filipino spirit. With the Philippine flag flying proudly behind her, ESL welcomes guests to the joint inauguration of Kita Corporation and Clark Plastic Manufacturing (CPM) Corporation.

Dr. Susumo Yoshida presents to ESL and Joseph Lim a plaque of appreciation from Aiwa Co., Ltd., on the inauguration of Kita Corp.. Close friend Freddie Santos hosts the occasion.

Aiwa TV products proudly Philippine-made. Joseph and Elena Lim with guests inside the Kita factory. Left to right: David S. Lim; Romeo David, President of Clark Development Corp.; Victor Lim, ESL, Dr. Susumo Yoshida, Senate President Edgardo Angara, Joseph Lim, Aiwa executives Mr. T. Iwai and Mr. H. Machida; Vincent Lim.

Kita Corporation Chairman Joseph Lim and Dr. Susumo Yoshida in front of the Kita entrance.

Tree of Hope. Dr. Susumo Yoshida plants inaugural tree while Joseph Lim, Senate President Edgardo Angara, and ESL look on.

ESL at the Kita Corporation plant in Clark touring New Zealand Trade Minister Philip Burdon and Canadian Ambassador Colin Bell.

ESL with New Zealand Ambassador Colin Bell, Rene Concepcion, Head of the Philippines-New Zealand Business Council, and Canadian Trade Minister Philip Burdon, during the group's visit to Kita Corporation.

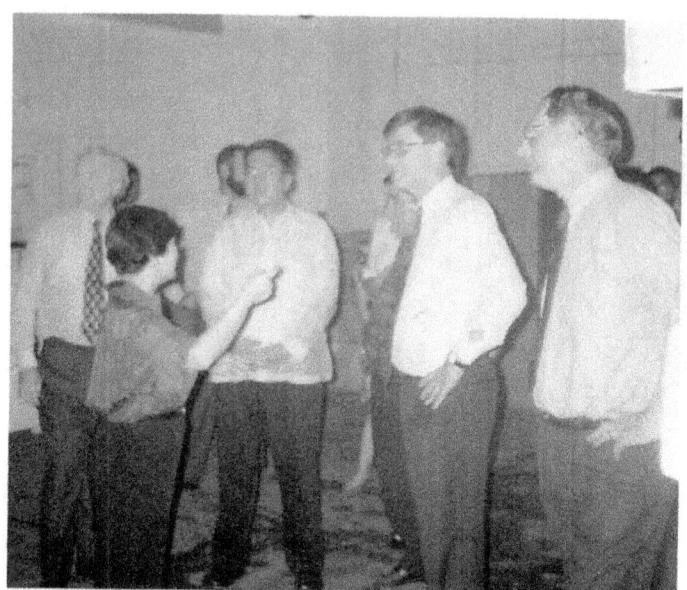

*ESL briefing visitors o[f]
the operations of Ki[ta]
Corporation's manufa[c]-
turing facilities. Left [to]
right: Ambassador Col[in]
Bell of New Zealan[d];
Rene Concepcion; Trad[e]
Minister Philip Burd[on]
of New Zealand.*

The sprawling complex of Kita Corporation.

Happy smiles from executives and guests of Clark Plastic Manufacturing (CPM) Corp. during CPM's inauguration. Standing from left to right: Cholo Baviera, Dennis Sy-Santos, Fidel Escario, Jr., George Tan, Local Government Secretary Raffy Alunan, Lita Joaquin, Susan L. Tan, Delfin Prospero. Seated from left to right: Beda Manalac, Leila Tan, Criselda Garcia, and Roehl Dumlao.

Executives of Kita, CPM, and Aiwa standing in front of state-of-the-art plastic injection machines of CPM. Left to right: Susan L. Tan, Joseph Lim, Dr. Susumo Yoshida, ESL, Senate President Edgardo Angara, H. Machida, Gar Lugtu, T. Iwai, Ricky Ligeralde, and David Lim.

After a worldwide search for top women executives, ESL was the only Filipino industrialist included in Worldbusiness Magazine's list of 50 WORLD-CLASS EXECUTIVES. Shown are the trophy and magazine issue marking the award.

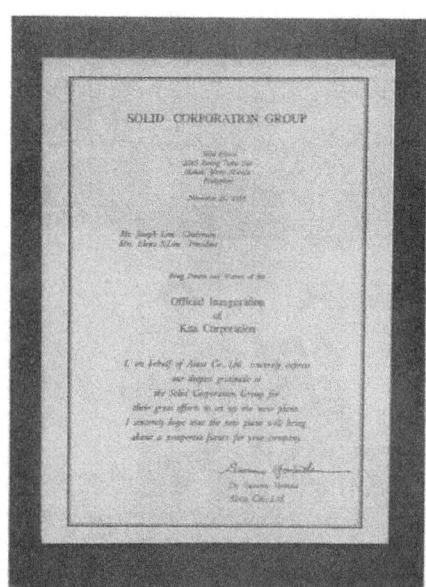

Plaque of appreciation from Aiwa Co., Ltd., on the inauguration of Kita Corporation.

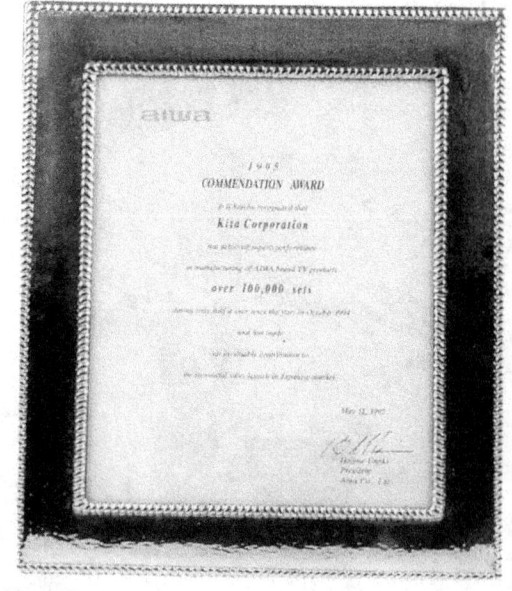

Kita Corporation passes the first acid test in the manufacturing of TV products: production of more than 100,000 sets. In honor of the achievement, Aiwa Co., Ltd., gave Kita Corp. a commendation award.

Doting grandmother celebrates birthday with her 10 grandchildren. Left to right: Melissa, Michelle, C.J., Isa, Meggy, Marvin, Kevin, Matthew, J.J., and Michael.

Meggy and Michelle. The future Elenas.

Chapter Five

Laguna International Industrial Park, Inc.

COURAGE AMIDST TURBULENCE

The Laguna International Industrial Park, Inc. (LIIP) represents an investment in a world-class industrial estate for foreign investors interested in setting up their factories in the Philippines.

It is the pioneer industrial estate established in Laguna in the early summer of 1990, just a few months after the most critical military coup attempt of December 1989.

LIIP covers 117 hectares located at Ganado and Mamplasan, Biñan, Laguna. All lot areas have been fully sold out — and inquiries from interested buyers still keep pouring in.

The factories at LIIP produce a wide range of products both for export and domestic sale.

It is the only industrial estate that constructed — and donated to the government — a huge public interchange called the Biñan Interchange. Its pioneering role in a most uncertain period is an act of faith. It ushered in more estates in the subsequent years. Today there are five other industrial estates in the Calabarzon area.

At 9:05 P.M. on February 25, 1986,

from my apartment on Paz Street, Paco, Manila, which is very near Malacañang Palace, I saw helicopters hovering over the presidential palace. I knew then that President Ferdinand Marcos, his family and close relatives, were being airlifted by the Americans to Clark Air Base (then still a US military facility).

It was the climax of the four-day EDSA "People's Power" Revolution. As a stunned world watched, Filipinos regained democracy through peaceful mass actions and prayers instead of bullets, putting an end to 20 years of Marcos' strongman rule over the country.

It also marked the beginning of several years of political and economic turbulence that affected all Filipinos. And it was in such a troubled environment that LIIP was born.

Corazon C. Aquino

became the next President. Shortly thereafter, President Aquino declared a revolutionary government in lieu of a democracy.

She appointed 50 men and women to draft the 1987 Constitution which was then submitted to the Filipino people for approval through a plebiscite. The people ratified the new Constitution which allowed her to stay in office without an election up to June 15, 1992. In effect she was given six years and four months in office.

There was euphoria and high expectations for the new government to give the people a better life. Everybody looked to a government that would be the exact opposite of that of President Marcos. People longed for justice, decency, level playing field in business and service, end of corruption and poor basic services, restoration of efficiency, effectiveness in government services, but above all a return to integrity in the lives and ways of the Filipino leadership.

But a sector of the military was disillusioned. It perceived President Aquino's rule as inept and even more corrupt than its predecessor. A liberal press unleashed its unbridled criticism against Mrs. Aquino's relatives who were alleged to be enriching themselves and taking advantage of their newly found powers and positions.

The first coup attempt
took place in 1987, followed by several others.

One coup had a comical character to it. The rebels took over the Manila Hotel and the Vice Presidential candidate of Mr. Marcos, Arturo Tolentino, was installed President.

The rebels were persuaded to surrender by Lt. Gen. Salvador Mison who talked them out of their plot. The rebels surrendered. As punishment, they were made to do some push-ups and were restored to their former positions after rejoining the armed forces.

Late in 1987,
Mr. Pil Kun Rhee, then Managing Director (now President) of Samsung Co., Ltd., of Korea, discussed with me, as CEO of the Solid Group of Companies (SGC), the possibility of setting up an industrial estate in the Philippines that would provide foreign investors with an attractive alternative site for their factories.

The business rationale was clear: Many foreign investors were interested in doing business in the Philippines but were discouraged by the lack of industrial sites that could meet their prerequisites in terms of infrastructure, power and water supply, telecommunication facilities, and human resources.

It would be located in the CALABARZON (or Cavite-Laguna-Batangas-Rizal-Quezon) Area, an aggrupation of contiguous provinces envisioned to spearhead Philippine industrialization. At that time, the only industrial estate of note in CALABARZON was the First Cavite Industrial Estate, a joint venture of the government with Maruberi, a Japanese company. Thus, there was a clear need for additional industrial estates.

Seeing the idea's soundness plus the tremendous boost the project would give to the Philippines' development efforts, I readily agreed to the Samsung proposal. This resulted in a massive hunt for the right location which took many of my managers to visit many areas in Cavite, Laguna, and Batangas. So many proposals. So many visits.

Then on December 2, 1989,
the military rebels struck again. This time, they took over strategic tall buildings as their position of defense in Makati, the heart of the nation's financial center.

There were shooting and sniping but it seemed the soldiers on the government side were shooting in the air because the bullets never seemed to hit the rebels and vice-versa. Again, the rebels were persuaded to return to their camps. This time there were no push-ups. The rebels were allowed to keep their weapons and they marched back to their camps.

After this, everything deteriorated.

The whole economy stood still. No investor was interested in the Philippines. The country was unstable. Overnight, real estate prices dropped. Factories cut down their operations.

The market was dull. What used to be a bright future faded with the last coup.

Under this gloom, I persisted in persuading Samsung Corporation to continue with our earlier agreement to form a joint venture for the development of the very first industrial estate in Laguna for the purpose of attracting Korean investors to move their factories to the Philippines. Aside from the Koreans, we also had other potential investors — Japanese, Filipinos, and other foreign nationals.

It was essential that we continue the project even under a most unfavorable business climate if only to reaffirm our faith in our country and people. To me, it was the challenge of the moment. The path of lesser resistance would have been to drop the whole project and wait for a more stable year. At this period, most if not all big projects were put on hold and a wait-and-see attitude permeated the air.

It is innate in me

to always challenge danger, to conquer the risk, to persist in my vision. If I fail, it will be due not to my fear, but to my heart not being strong enough to overcome the fear.

Virtually no one else wanted to invest. Everyone was waiting for a more opportune moment. I could also have played safe, but I chose to dare. I practically guaranteed the success of the project to my Korean partner. I showed them my good faith by advancing all the preparatory logistics to the consolidators who, in turn, guaranteed the same success. It was primarily having the will and faith to succeed.

Amidst this negative economic growth and weak credibility of the country, I pushed for this project. To me, it meant a great deal to show that despite the recent coup, despite the "wait-and-see" attitude of the business sector, despite the waning confidence of many, someone was willing to invest and show trust, to lead and believe.

Finally, Samsung gave in

to my endless pitching, but under very stringent conditions for me.

One condition was that our start-up budget for the venture would be 10 million pesos — the entire amount to be advanced by Solid, 50 per cent to be reimbursed later by Samsung in case the project fell through.

The other condition from my end was that someone other than me would handle the headaches of dealing with government and the farmers whose lots we would purchase.

I set the latter condition because I felt I was not competent to negotiate with the farmers, nor did I have the experience and energy to go through government's bureaucratic maze in matters pertaining to land acquisition. This is best left to the expert consultants in this activity. To this condition, Samsung likewise agreed.

So we entrusted the purchase of the land to JMT, a consulting company engaged in consolidating, packaging, documenting, and effecting smooth acquisition of properties in a strictly proper and legal manner. We entered into an agreement with JMT for this purpose.

We paid

two-hundred-pesos (P200.00) per square meter: P100.00/ sq.m. for the farmers and another P100.00/sq.m. to the consulting firm as "total consulting and packaging fee."

Under the latter, the consultants were to discharge the following functions: locate the site suitable for the industrial estate purpose, negotiate with the farmers, consolidate the numerous existing titles and get new titles, work out all government approvals, coordinate the farmers' relocation to new homelots, and do any necessary act for the final turnover of the property free from all liens and encumbrances.

The P200.00/sq.m. was a stiff price considering that the going rate then was only P50.00 to P70.00/sq.m. for the land. But I was willing to pay it because I wanted the farmers to earn more, as well as have a consulting firm who could take care of negotiations with the farmers and government, and handle all the documentation until final completion. Since this was the first time an industrial estate would be put up in Laguna, we wanted to ensure a "botherless" process for us. We would only take over when everything was completed and start the actual civil works, also through contractors.

It was a pioneer effort;

at that time, there was nobody putting up an industrial estate in Laguna, so there were many unforeseen elements.

While the government talked of "build-operate-transfer" (BOT), there were no guidelines for BOT.

Another problem was with the Department of Agrarian Reform (DAR). The area we wanted to purchase was part of the real estate property supposedly owned by former President Marcos which was surrendered to the Aquino administration's Presidential Commission on Good Goverment (PCGG). In turn, PCGG gave the titles to the DAR, and the latter gave the land to agrarian reform beneficiaries. Thus, we needed to get approval from DAR for the conversion of the area into an industrial estate.

But DAR did not have clear guidelines then regarding the conversion process. This was the stage when they were still formulating their guidelines. JMT was at the forefront of all these activities and at this point in time, I realized that we had already exceeded the P10 million budget and JMT still had not completed the approval process. The P10 million was spent by the consolidating company, JMT, for the process of consolidation and negotiations with the farmers, as well as for advances to the farmers for the latter's subsistence while this was going on.

To stop right there and then would mean a total loss of the P10 million. But I wasn't thinking of the P10 million. I was thinking of the loss of the opportunity. How can we complete this if we are bogged down after spending the whole amount agreed upon with Samsung.

So it reached a point wherein I had to make a decision whether to advance additional amounts or not. If I didn't advance the money, the project was dead because the Koreans could not advance it. Samsung, being a very large company, had to go through the government process before they could bring in any money. So it was our company that advanced the P10 million. We agreed on this amount on the assurance that this would cover what JMT needed to complete all negotiations and legal requirements.

The JMT consolidators begged me
to have an audience with the farmers. And I refused. "Our contract is for you to package everything. I don't want to be talking to farmers because it is so difficult to talk to more than 250 farmers for that small property."

"But it will not be 250," they assured me. "There will be only about six farmers who will represent the entire group."

So very reluctantly, I agreed to talk to the representatives. And the talk was all about their request that I pay them ten-thousand pesos (P10,000.00) a month while waiting for government approval for the purchase of the area. I said, "How can I give you P10,000.00 a month per family when your land is so small, and even if you were to plant for one year, you cannot even get P10,000.00 a year. So don't you think it is too much? I don't think I can meet your requirement. Let us call this whole thing off."

I was willing to call the whole thing off

at that point because I thought I was getting unreasonable demands.

But finally, they settled for a much lesser amount. All their advances reached to a very substantial sum. And had it been disapproved by the DAR, I myself would have personally lost millions of pesos. The only "reimbursement" would be the P5 million rebate of Samsung.

But I took a chance because I felt that the country needed it. Considering that it was the period right after the disastrous 1989 coup, I felt that, more than any other time, I should show my confidence, faith, and help rebuild the credibility of the Philippines.

So finally, after one year, the whole thing was approved. It was a process that lasted for a year, and I thought, this is quite a tedious process because it had to go through the approval of the Municipal Agrarian Reform Office (MARO), Provincial Agrarian Reform Office (PARO), Regional Agrarian Reform Office (RARO), the Department of Agrarian Reform head agency, and 23 other agencies in the government!

But by then, the atmosphere was still not good for investment. This was in 1991. It was still a very low stage in the economy because while there were lots of talk about economic recovery, we were plagued by endless daily brownouts. How can you recover without electricity? It was really only during the Ramos administration after 1993 that the power problem was solved and we began to have rapid acceleration of growth. But that period was really a pitiful economic period in our country.

Immediately upon getting government approval, the development of the property went into high gear. Debris was cleared; sewer/water/power/communication systems were installed, roads were built.

Then the bombshell:
after one year of intensive site development, we received a letter from the DAR Secretary informing us that DAR was revoking its approval on our acquisition of the entire area.

This was shocking and crazy, to say the least. Everything was already in place. We were almost through with all the main construction work.

JMT immediately went to DAR to find out the cause of the revocation. After some months, JMT requested me to have lunch with the DAR Secretary, upon the latter's invitation.

This was the very first time
that I met a DAR executive and no less than the Secretary.

Well, facing the DAR Secretary, I asked him what was wrong with the conversion.

"Nothing is wrong," he replied. "Only that it was signed by a DAR regional director and not by an undersecretary."

I countered: "Is it illegal? Are we supposed to know that the approval has to be signed by an undersecretary?"

He answered, "No, no, no. We have an internal memo that instructs conversion above five hectares has to be signed by a DAR undersecretary. Anyway, it can easily be cured."

"How do we 'cure'? What are we supposed to do?"

"Oh, just make a letter of reconsideration."

"Well, how long will it take? You know I have foreign partners here. They have relied upon the correctness of the process. It took us a year to go through the approval of the 23 government agencies. How much longer do we have to wait?

"My Korean partners are very edgy about this. I convinced them to invest here and to transfer their technology here and now we already have Korean investors ready to come in. Time is of the essence. We should not lose this opportunity now that we have them already."

At that time, very few people wanted to invest in the Philippines. The DAR Secretary assured me that the problem would be "cured" in a week or two. At most, a month. So I was very happy about it, and I went home and I told my consultants the Secretary's promise. "So you work on it," I ordered them.

They did work on it. But

things did not work because the Secretary cured it by sitting on it for another year. And I had to write letters to President Aquino asking her "Are you sincere about inviting investors? Because if you are not sincere, we should have been told ahead. Then I would not have gone into this."

I had already taken so many risks to show faith in the country and now, we had a ridiculous situation of having a previous approval revoked because of a technicality that among those that were approved, there were three pieces of titles that were five hectares and above. But these titles had co-owners of more than 80 farmers. So if they were going to divide these five hectares into the number of co-owners, it would turn out that every farmer would own only 3,000 to 4,000 square meters. So if a director can sign for less than five hectares for one owner, what is the logic there that he cannot sign an area more than five hectares but where each co-owner actually owns only 3,000 to 4,000 square meters?

Anyway, after one long year of waiting, the same Secretary who revoked it finally approved our acquisition.

Shortly after we got the final approval, construction was completed. But now we had a new problem. This was in late 1991 and it seemed investors were still too scared to come in because of the nation's perceived instability. In fact, by this time, there were also several industrial estates being put up in the Calabarzon area and they too had difficulty getting investors.

We were almost getting mosquitoes as clients
because very few were asking about land and how to invest their property.

So all of us felt we went into the wrong business. The same thing happened to the adjoining industrial estate which came in a year later. They, too, felt the difficulty of marketing their lots for investments, for export sales and domestic sales.

"Mother of All Land Scams!"
As though the trials we had gone through were not enough, one day we suddenly woke up to front-page headlines in national newspapers that proclaimed Elena Lim's Laguna

Industrial Estate as the "Mother of all Land Scams."

These headlines were based on a statement by a certain public official. I was in Hong Kong when this happened. I sent him a letter asking him what this was all about. How did it become the "Mother of all Land Scams?"

Later on, the official wrote me a letter which was a semi-apology and he also denied ever having made the accusation that LIIP was the "Mother of all Land Scams." Now, whether media invented the charge or not, the damage was done. The damage was that it frightened all the investors. After all, who would want to invest in the "Mother of All Land Scams?"

As expected, senators and congressmen

pounced on the issue. A certain senator called for a Senate hearing.

There were about three senators present during the hearing. Some of the farmers also came.

I explained the whole procedure, how we acquired the land, how we conformed; why it was even derailed for one year. I gave all the reasons which they found satisfactory.

There were some farmers who said that we promised a small schoolhouse for the children, a basketball court, and they were not still there. But it was explained that all these have nothing to do with the purchases. They are additions to what we will do for the community. We are just helping them. And in fact, we complied with all of them. Furthermore, in building this industrial estate we did something which no one ever did.

First, we built and donated a barangay road at our expense of more than 2.8 kilometers.

Then we constructed an interchange that connected

the whole Biñan area to our estate as well as to the main highway at a cost of one-hundred-forty million pesos (P140,000,000.00).

Then we donated the P140 million

interchange to government with absolutely nothing in exchange.

We did not avail of government's "Build-Operate-Transfer" (BOT) scheme which would have enabled us to recover our advance for this interchange. Because at that time, asking for the BOT guidelines would most likely mean delaying the LIIP project by another year or so. In our eagerness to have entry and exit access, we were willing to donate it to the government — which we did. And today, the Toll Regulatory Board collects P6.50 for every vehicle that goes in and out of that interchange which we built, earning millions for the government in the many years it will be collecting tolls.

Then it was the congressmen's turn.

Hardly were we over with the Senate hearing than we received a summons from the House of Representatives for the same hearing. And again, we presented before the House the argument and the whole thing was a repetition of the Senate hearing.

It became a convoluted hearing because it was not zeroed in on our estate but it brought in all the complaints of all the farmers around the area. Even farmers who were cheated out of their land by other people. And so, it was not a hearing that would bring anything in aid of legislation.

We immediately lost 15 major Korean investors

and hundreds of potential jobs for Filipino workers, thanks to that controversy.

The Koreans had already made a small downpayment of 10% for their planned factory sites at LIIP. They withdrew their downpayment and decided to invest in another country.

Who knows what economic benefits those Koreans who left could have given the nation? I still fume when I think about all the opportunities we lost due to the smallness of some people's minds.

After a derailment of three years,

we renewed our campaign to attract investors.

But it was only in 1994 when electrical power was fully restored and confidence was built up under the Ramos Administration that we were able to convince more investors to set up shop at LIIP.

The good news is that today, LIIP has been fully sold out, and we still get so many inquiries from new investors who want to build their factories at LIIP.

In hindsight, the LIIP experience

offers many lessons for entrepreneurs because it shows the interplay of a very broad spectrum of Philippine society: farmers; lawyers; mass media; the executive, legislative, and judicial branches of government; foreign and local investors — even military rebels!

The excruciatingly convoluted twists and turns of the LIIP story should be fair warning to every aspiring entrepreneur about the stuff he or she must be made of to succeed in entrepreneurship. In dealing with so many persons, institutions, and factors, the entrepreneur must develop the courage, wisdom, and strength to handle countless problems and surprises.

But the vital lesson,
I think, is that we should help our country not only in good times but, most importantly, in bad times.

It is easy to make large investments when there's hardly any risk. But as Filipino entrepreneurs, it is in our nation's darkest hours when we must keep the faith.

And take the leap of faith.

Chapter Six

Sumida Electric (Phils.), Inc.

BRIGHT BEGINNING, DARK END

"United we stand, divided we fall"

Everything looked bright,
that afternoon in 1989, when the idea of a partnership with Sumida Electric (Far East) was born.

I was then in a meeting with Mr. S. Yawata, the Managing Director of Sumida Electric (Far East) Ltd. . We were in my office at the old Solid Building at T.M. Kalaw, Ermita, Manila.

"How would you like to be our partner, Mrs. Lim?" The offer from Mr. Yawata came without warning, taking me completely by surprise.

My mind
was in a whirl as I pondered on his offer.

The Philippine economy was just resurging from the shambles of the failed Marcos regime and the after-effects of the EDSA Revolution. My hands were full of all kinds of problems: marketing uncertainties, parts sourcing difficulties due to the unstable economic condition, labor unrest as evidenced by the sudden surge of strikes affecting many companies, including ours.

It was certainly not an encouraging environment to start a new business. But yet, the excitement of finally making it big in exports fascinated me. The production of this new project would be 100% exported. It was intimidating but exciting indeed!

I looked across the table
at my impeccably dressed, youthful, but nonetheless erudite-looking visitor.

Even as Mr. Yawata was waiting for my response, several thoughts were running in my mind.

I am no stranger to the world of electronic manufacturing, but this type of technology that Sumida represented was entirely new to me.

If I accept
his offer, would we be able to recruit enough people to run the company?

Would the inexperienced people we could hire cope with the demands of the job?

Would we be able to attract good management people to guide the company's destiny?

Would Filipino managers and production workers be able to relate to expatriate bosses of diverse cultures?

Would we be able to handle a workforce of 2,000 workers in the next three years without any labor problem?

Would we be able to put up the needed infrastructure in a compressed time of eight months?

Would we be able to guarantee the foreign investors and assure them of just-in-time delivery?

Would we be able to recruit, screen, train and qualify within two months the first 100 trainees to be sent overseas?

Deal or No Deal?

We had to decide on this question quickly. Time was of great essence. The demand and the opportunity were imminent. Failure to meet the challenge meant "no deal." The opportunity was a great challenge — a challenge to harness our energies into being able to meet Sumida's requirements. To do so, we had to:

1. Send off within 60 days 100 trainees overseas for 90 days training (and get ready passports, travel documents, parental consent, and the like).
2. Prepare the plans for the factory such as building/electrical/plumbing plans; order and import machinery and equipment within 90 days.
3. Obtain government registration and documentation in 30 days.
4. Recruit additional 300 workers in 90 days.
5. Apply and get approval from Meralco for our power requirements; get our power substation connected.
6. Plan production to meet export targets. And many others.

"I am flattered by your offer, but...,"

I replied. I realized that a "No" answer now would mean the transfer of this opportunity to either Malaysia or China which were originally considered for this expansion.

"Your group comes highly recommended, Mrs. Lim," Mr. Yawata interrupted gently. "You have distinguished yourselves in your field. My friend, the manager of Mitsui Bank in Hongkong, assured me of your firm's capability.

"He told me to take a look at the Philippines before I finally decide to expand our manufacturing facilities in either Malaysia or China. As I told you, our China operations employ about 4,000 persons and our Malaysia operations have over 2,000 employees.

"This business is both automated and yet very labor-intensive and we have to keep on researching and improving our products which we supply to our many customers who are mainly manufacturers of electronic products like cameras, TVs . . . We make several hundred kinds of coils, filters, mini-transformers, and the like.

"In this business, timing is very important. We must be able to read the business growth and prepare for the increases in demand that are forthcoming. However, any sudden drop in world demand for the end finished products would immediately affect us. It is very interesting and challenging but also risky, I guess, just like any other business."

"Mr. Yawata,"

I said, "your industry is indeed a very important component in the manufacture of electronic products. The quality of their products will depend on your precision parts or parts of parts.

"Actually, this type of industry is best suited for Filipinos who are highly intelligent, quick to learn and adapt, curious and adept in all kinds of work especially in the dexterity of hands and alertness of mind. I'm very positive that we can better the output of your workers in Malaysia or even China. We have an added advantage, too. We speak English and this makes communication easier."

Mr. Yawata said, "Well, I am not familiar with Filipino culture and talent. But you are from the

Philippines and you have succeeded very well in your manufacturing and distribution of Sony products here. I understand that you made Sony the No. 1 leader besting all the other good brands. To me, this is a very commendable achievement.

"But you must understand that our process is far more labor-intensive than what you are doing now. Our raw materials are tiny and need focus in their operations. We need accuracy and concentration. We need good teamwork in all areas of operations. We cannot afford to lose our customers due to parts defect, late delivery, poor quality, inaccurate count or packaging, delay in shipment caused by your pre-shipment inspection of the SGS."

The problem

of dealing with the *Societe Generale de Surveillance*, more commonly known as "SGS," was then raised by Mr Yawata.

SGS is a Swiss-based inspection company reputed to be one of the largest of its kind in the world. The Philippine government signed a contract authorizing them to make pre-shipment inspection and valuation . Inspection has its uses but it certainly does not make any sense in the case of exports.

"We understand that to ship parts to your country you require SGS Clean Report of Findings which requires us to notify SGS five days prior to shipment for them to do the inspection.

"This requirement will make our business untenable and definitely not possible to be efficient. Our parts shipment is daily by air both for outgoing finished parts and incoming raw materials. To subject them to SGS inspection will not be workable. I'm afraid that even if your people are excellent workers, this will not be enough for us to succeed."

"You are absolutely right, Mr. Yawata," I said. "The SGS will be a stumbling block. We will have to ask the government for exemption from the SGS pre-shipment inspection requirement. There is already a precedent here. The government has exempted the semi-conductors industry from SGS inspection for the bringing in of their parts and raw materials. Our parts are allied to and similar with those of the semi-conductor companies. We will not proceed with the final agreement until we get the exemption from the government.

"Nonetheless, we can proceed with the preparations for the project so that we can meet your time schedule. I assure you that you will not regret making the Philippines a good manufacturing base for your parts. Also, the consumer electronics products companies here are increasing their sales. In the future they will also be your customers for your parts. We have to be optimistic about these things. Me, I have all the faith and confidence that the Philippines will be a great manufacturing base. I'm certainly challenged.

"We'll talk more the next meeting after I've made more studies to meet all the demands of this business. Meanwhile, let me show you all the possible places where we can do this activity."

Thereafter, I showed Mr. Yawata several possible places. They all needed substantial renovations to be usable for the project.

True, he had come

to the country at the instigation of his friend, the manager of Mitsui Bank in Hongkong. It was clear that he wanted to expand Sumida's coil manufacturing operations in Asia.

Sumida already had plants operating in Japan, China, Taiwan, Hong Kong, Korea, and Malaysia. Mr. Yawata envisioned a network in the Far East that would pave the way for faster-filled rates of orders and, consequently, better customer service.

I knew I had given him ample information and reasons why foreign businessmen should invest in our country — reasons which focused on our well-educated manpower, our accessibility to major points in Asia, our awakening local economy, our developing capabilities in infrastructure and telecommunications, and the continuing pursuit for stability of our government. At that time, the aborted December 1989 coup d'etat had yet to happen, the great earthquake had yet to come, and the devastating Mt. Pinatubo eruption was still beyond reality.

Workers' compensation

was a major item I discussed with Mr. Yawata.

It had to be competitive and at the same time meet all labor laws

I have seen many companies who do not comply with labor laws so I always make it a policy that if I could not meet the requirements, then I should not go into such business. But here was an opportunity to be able to provide good jobs and with potentials of growth which will seep back to the workers' welfare, too.

Normally, new trainee-employees are paid apprentice rates during the first six months while undergoing training. But because of our business philosophy and value in always looking after the welfare of our workforce, we agreed to immediately hire them on probationary status to be regularized after six months without going through an apprenticeship phase.

I also got a concession from Mr. Yawata that even those who would train overseas would continue to receive the minimum wage which would be given to their families or authorized recipients.

Thus, aside from the normal pay, the trainees would be given free board and lodging. All these were fully discussed with Mr. Yawata to the benefit of our employees.

"We will take a chance

on putting our money and faith in your people, Mrs. Lim. We believe that we can succeed because of your good track record, strong determination to overcome problems, excellent workers, and good managerial organization. Okay! Let's shake hands and do business."

So with a handshake, I agreed to go into business to supply coils to Sumida-Far East. The formal agreements were drafted later on to document our discussions.

Mr. Yawata was clearly enthusiastic about our project. He was surely not the traditional Japanese executive who usually is very reticent, cautious, conservative and very partial to their interests first. He represented a new breed of young executives trained in the United States and influenced greatly by British liberality, yet fully imbibed in Japanese culture and history. He combined the best of Asian and Western worlds. He possessed long-term vision and, certainly, was very people-oriented. We had hardly started our joint venture when already his vision was going ahead of time.

"I envision

a world-class training facility here in the Philippines. We shall conduct management and development courses for Sumida officers worldwide and technical courses, too, for other employees," Mr. Yawata intruded into my thoughts softly. "We shall call it 'The Sumida School of Management (Philippines).' How about it?"

"I am enamoured by the thought," I replied, looking straight into his eyes. "Did you know that by inclination and first choice, I am a teacher before anything else? I spent seven years of my early adulthood teaching three levels of studies, from kindergarten to high school and college. Mr. Yawata, if what you envision is realized, it will really be a great dream come true for me, perhaps even much more than my present businesses in terms of number of beneficiaries and development potential.

"I have always longed to be a potent part of the education, especially technical and management, that would provide tools for our young people to become active and valuable citizens contributing to nation-building."

We were both very excited

about the Sumida Management and Training School in the Philippines. I offered my six-storey building in Manila for this purpose. We envisioned monthly management meetings with all Sumida managers coming from Hong Kong, Japan, China, Malaysia, Taiwan, and Korea.

The School would be an excellent source of information and education, cohesive cooperation, and intimate bonding for the exchange of ideas, dialogues, seminars, post-audit exercises, and growth development and sustenance in school.

We talked about converting two or three floors of the building for dormitory and hotel-like accommodations for all the Senior Managers. The building at the top floor even had facilities for basketball, badminton, volleyball, sauna, and game rooms.

Now, more than ever,

I had to give greater effort to make our project succeed for this special dream to come true — a dream that would employ 2,000 workers, earn much needed foreign exchange, gain valuable technology, add revenues to government's coffers, and, lastly, provide the opportunity for me to instill ethical behaviour and good values to our employees. Indeed, a wonderful dream!

"But first, we must have our production started at the earliest possible time." he continued. "Will your people be ready in, say, about six months? We will give you a hundred percent technical assistance."

I nodded my assent. "So be it," I heard myself reply even as my head was swimming with the enormity of the deed. I knew I had to because it would create many jobs for Filipinos and provide an example to other foreign investors who might be having second thoughts of investing in the Philippines. The entrepreneur in me replied, committing myself to procuring government approvals, readying production facilities, recruiting, training people and shipping the products all in the short span of six to eight months.

Boldly I dreamed

to manufacture millions of coils, filters, and mini-transformers in the first two years with a thousand employees . . . to initially locate the plant at the former Delta Motor factory along South Superhighway . . . then to build a new plant at the Laguna International Industrial Park which would be the permanent home of the factory.

I envisioned that by the third year, we would be hiring another thousand employees to double our capacity. This would be at the same level as the Sumida Plant in China when it was established four years earlier. (Today, Sumida-China has over 6,000 employees.)

I dreamed that Sumida-Philippines would prove to be the best Sumida plant in Asia. I believed in my dream because of my strong faith and trust in the Filipino capability, competence, and integrity.

By the middle

of the second year, actual developments were proving my vision correct. The training proceeded excellently. The flexibility and output were satisfactory. The focus, dedication, and commitment to strengthen our competencies were all present. How could I fail?

Plans were being drawn up for the construction of the Sumida plant in Laguna. We expected the plant to be fully constructed in six months. I was doing a lot of preparatory meetings and consultations with the architects and contractors.

Mr. Yawata was so impressed with our boldness, enthusiasm and fortitude in investing all infrastructural requirements in Laguna that he, too, believed that there was no reason why the Sumida (Phils.) plant would not perform as well as the older plants in China, Malaysia, and Taiwan.

Our dreams became

an immediate reality after October 16, 1989, the birth of Sumida Electric (Phils.), Inc. (SEPI). We established the SEPI office and factory along South Expressway in La Huerta, Paranaque.

Our family's Solid Corporation owned SEPI. It was, therefore, a Filipino entity from the very start. We adopted the name "Sumida (Phils.), Inc." to enhance the corporate identity as a part of the Sumida Group and inspire confidence from Sumida's worldwide customers.

Unfortunately, this issue was never clarified to the employees by our managers. This resulted in the erroneous consensus that SEPI was part of and owned by that large multinational organization. This vague notion that SEPI was owned by Sumida Group contributed to the events that happened later on.

We registered the company with the BOI as a non-pioneer enterprise operating under the Omnibus Investments Code of 1989. As a purely exporting company, SEPI was entitled to certain tax and non-tax incentives.

We felt then that nothing could stop us from pursuing our vision. We had the political will and sense of urgency to get things done.

On my part, I did all that it took to get the job done. With passion and intelligent emotion, I moved paper, people, and property.

According to our contract

with Sumida (Far East), SEPI production materials, tools, factory machineries and equipment, and vehicles all belonged to Sumida (FE) and were only consigned to SEPI for as long as production continued.

All other assets that were needed to run the business, including the building and improvements, were owned by SEPI. All expenses that were incurred to operate the business were all for the account of SEPI. In other words, SEPI was entirely dependent on Sumida (FE) for its business.

Sumida (FE) was both SEPI's raw materials and technology supplier and lone customer. They provided us all the technical know-how and raw materials for making the filters, coil capacitors, mini-transformers, etc., and then they bought back all the finished parts for delivery to their customers in Japan, China, Malaysia, Thailand, Singapore, the U.S. and Europe.

In a way, it was a contractual agreement with the deviation that we owned the factory building and paid for all the operating expenses, and provided for all the manpower requirements. In return, we were paid for the job. Actually, this kind of operation is favorable to the workers because they learn the skills and are outrightly paid reasonable decent wages plus overtime and are working in fully airconditioned premises. All the training costs, both foreign and local. are fully absorbed by the company.

The unemployment problem

was underscored by the number of applicants who answered our want ads.

"Next!" You could hear the security guard calling out during those early hectic days of recruiting the workforce. "Next!" He would holler even as he motioned to an applicant to stand alongside the measuring mark.

It was the easiest way I could think of to screen early applicants for the SEPI factory. We did not anticipate the large number of applicants. Almost a thousand applied for the assembly worker and supervisory and engineering positions. Their line stretched the entire length of Churruca St. in Ermita, Manila, at the back of the Solid Building.

Since SEPI assembly work would be linear and segmental, I decided to hire workers that would roughly be of the same height range for their own convenience. Thus, I ordered the measuring mark to be painted along the Churruca side of the building. From there, the applicants were instructed to proceed upstairs to the

Personnel Department for interview and psychological as well as simple IQ and attitude tests, aside from manual dexterity samplings.

Eventually, we recruited around a hundred people. Except for a sprinkling of engineers and new managers, most of the recruits were high school graduates with no experience in any electronic-type of production work. It was the first job for most of them, having just graduated from high school.

We deemed it necessary, therefore, to send 90 of them to Sumida-China for three months training before starting operations. This stemmed from the lack of training facilities here that are comparable to the depth and speed of training available in Sumida's China factory. Also, this was the best way to fast-track the training.

A very generous
act was done by Mr. Yawata during their stay in China. "I shall give them US$3.00 daily allowance for their small personal needs," he jubilantly told me. This was something extra because all of them brought their own pocket money.

"That is quite generous of you." I was taken by surprise but pleased nonetheless at this special concession on his part. "That will add to their daily peso allowance or, rather, minimum wage advance payment here." Surely, I thought to myself, that should be added incentive for our workers to value their jobs.

But despite their benefits,
the trainees turned out to be picky. They complained about the Chinese food served in the cafeteria which normally consisted of rice, vegetables, two kinds of viands, and tea. They mentioned that they were tired of the same kind of cooking.

To remedy this situation, we arranged for them to eat the same food as the Japanese managers in the same dining area.

Of course, the Chinese workers felt slighted. After all, they were in their own country yet they were seemingly discriminated against. None of us were to blame, however, since not even Mr. Yawata had any control over their working conditions. Only their Communist Chinese Government had any say over them. Poor Chinese workers! Compared to them, our trainees had it made.

Mr. Yawata did all he could to make their training comfortable and profitable. He provided them free board and lodging plus uniforms and a travelling bag to put their things in. Compared to the Chinese workers who slept eight to a room, our trainees slept four to a room. This, too, added to the strained relationship between the Chinese workers and our trainees.

The trainees were also allowed a weekly Karaoke session to ward off loneliness. On top of this, during Sundays transportation was provided to bring them to church. This was no small concession on our part considering the distance they had to travel from the factory to the church and back. At Christmas, we sent them home to the Philippines so they could enjoy the holiday season with their families. We even allowed them to pass through Hong Kong to shop.

"Try not to blow away

all of your hard-earned daily allowances on *pasalubongs* (homecoming gifts) alone," I admonished them.

When one is in Hong Kong the first time, however, that is easier said than done. Our trainees were on Cloud 9. Not only were they given time to shop, they were also feted to dinner at one of Hong Kong's swank restaurants, compliments of Mr. Yawata.

In hindsight, I believe it was a case of our trainees having too much too soon which might have inflated their egos making them vulnerable to exploitation by union organizers.

They believed they could bend the company to accede to any demand they might make, reasonable or not. On the other hand, we could not refuse to give them those benefits because it is one of our company policies to value the human being as a very important part of our organization who must be given good working conditions so that they in turn will give the best of themselves to the work at hand.

While the 90 recruits

were training in China, we were kept very busy here in Manila with the nitty-gritty details of renovating factory space, laying out machineries on the factory floor including generators that were a basic necessity due to the inevitable brownouts then prevailing.

We also had to put up a substation for the power line to get in. Needless to say, these incurred quite an expense. All these, added to the paper chase at government offices, kept me on my toes. Applying at various government offices for all kinds of permits seemed endless and very taxing.

One particular exemption we applied for gave us lots of problems. This was the application for exemption from SGS pre-shipment inspection which we filed with the Department of Trade & Industry that needed the approval of the Central Bank's Monetary Board.

"Don't they realize that the essence of survival of the export-oriented businesses especially of the fast-moving electronic sector is timely delivery?" I would often bemoan to myself.

Evidently, the SGS is not overly concerned whether you are hassled by delays or not. So if you think that applying for an exemption from SGS inspection is easy, think again. It is not a task for the faint-hearted entrepreneur. The government's prescribed process is to let one go the entire gamut of approvals — from the inter-agency committee to the Department of Trade and Industry, the Department of Finance, the Board of Investments, and the Central Bank — a task which usually takes no less than six months. An exercise in wasting time.

We certainly had problems

right from the very start. One crucial DTI director outrightly denied our application, saying that the regulations allow only semi-conductor companies to be exempted from SGS inspection which we so badly needed.

"How come?" I asked.

"Well, only semi-conductor companies are allowed under the regulation since their fast-moving export of parts need to be delivered to companies abroad at the shortest possible time and because there is no local market for semi-conductors," was his answer.

"And you think that my products, coils and filters, do not fall under the same category of the regulation?" I countered.

"The regulation states specifically that only semi-conductors," he stressed the word as he looked sympathetically at me, "be given this privilege." And he pointed to a chart of semi-conductor parts on the wall behind his desk.

"Don't you realize that if our raw materials are tied up with SGS inspection, our deliveries would be delayed and that would be the end of our venture?" I pleaded.

"Regulation is regulation." Sympathetic futility echoed in his voice.

"You expect us to give SGS at least five days notice prior to inspection and shipment. That's totally out of the question since our materials are airlifted at least three times weekly, if not daily. That's why we need this exemption." I was totally flabbergasted with this kind of strait jacket mentality of bureaucrats. It's a regulation- oriented system. Can you imagine a great opportunity like this going to be wasted on a silly rule?

I knew it was useless
to reason with a one-track-minded government official who follows perceived rules to the letter. My experience in dealing with government officials has familiarized me with such a bureaucratic and one-track attitude which, unfortunately, is the norm of public service. These are the kind of deterrents that can easily discourage an entrepreneur unless he has the guts to deal with them resourcefully. He must also have the determination to succeed notwithstanding any barrier.

I asked for a copy of the debatable regulation. He was kind enough to tell me to go to the Central Bank which is the final approving body. It turned out that an exemption of this kind needed the endorsement of the secretaries of Finance and the DTI and the approval of the entire Monetary Board! If this was not crimson red tape, what could be worse?

Hurrying to the Central Bank,

I sought the help of the Director of the CICCO who referred me to one of his lower staff. There, I was likewise told that the exemption is only limited to semi-conductor companies as this was requested by their association after the implementation of SGS pre-shipment inspection scheme. These semi-conductor companies are all owned by multinationals. In our system, it is easier for such an association to be heard and favorably acted upon.

I was very vehement in my opposition to the services of the SGS which I believe up to now restrains trade, causes many lost opportunities, breeds corruption, and, worst, demeans our sense of worth and dignity as a people able to manage their own affairs.

Inspection and valuation of goods are mandates inherent in our laws to be performed by our customs personnel. Engaging the services of a foreign firm for a fee to do this duty is absolutely untenable. Here in this case is a clear example how an SGS presence would have aborted this export business had I not personally, persistently, and resourcefully followed through the application.

I requested to see the so-called regulation limiting the exemption only to semi-conductor companies. I read the pertinent paragraphs and — Eureka! — found it. The solution to my problem was right there in their own rules, which dispositive portion shows that SGS exemption is allowed to semi-conductors and other allied products.

"Here," I pointed out rather gleefully, "does this not mean that you may consider Sumida Philippines products which are coils, filters, transistors, etcetera as part of those allied products?"

True to character, he still said, "No!

Had I been a greenhorn

in the business or less persevering, I might have taken his answer as gospel truth and given up. Wouldn't you? It was like a blank wall that was suddenly put up before me. But I've never taken "No" for an answer when my objective is clear before me — the objective of getting Sumida-Philippines on the move. I turned on my heels and left.

Again, I questioned in my mind our government's policy of encouraging local entrepreneurs on one hand, and smothering them on the other by making it difficult for them to obtain all kinds of approvals and licenses. What kind of public officials do we have that they can't see beyond the mere letter of the law to apply its real spirit? I gritted my teeth to think our taxes pay these bureaucrats who turn out not to be helpful or understanding when we need them.

There was no sense, however, in wallowing in self-pity. I had to view the problem as a challenge. I knew there was still one recourse left. DTI top man Secretary Jose "Joe" Concepcion, Jr., himself. Immediately, I sought an audience with him.

Great was my relief

when Secretary Concepcion rose to the challenge of the hour.

"You mean to tell me the processes for these filters, coils, and capacitors are similar to the semi-conductors' components?" It was something new to him.

"Yes, Mr. Secretary, they are. Our coils are 12mm as finished products." I showed him pictures to substantiate my claim.

"And your market is . . ."

"Not here, sir. There is no market for these products here. They're all destined for export. The business of Sumida-Philippines has exactly the same demands as the semi-conductor industry. We need our raw materials as fast as they do, too. If you can make a concession to the semi-conductor industry, why not to an allied industry?" I was impassioned in my plea. "Just think, this is it! There'll be jobs for our people, technology to be learned, export revenues to be earned."

"You've proven your point," the Secretary finally said. "I'm convinced." And he called his subordinate, the DTI Director.

"I'll ask only one question," he told him. "Do these parts have any market here?" I didn't expect the Secretary to be so angry, but he was so livid with anger when there was no response from the man before him. "Do these products have any market here?" This time there was thunder in the Secretary's voice.

"None, sir," was the meek reply.

"Then, is there any reason why we should deny the application for exemption from SGS inspection?" and he thumped the copy of our application with a hard hand.

"None, sir," the officious official conceded.

"Then have the resolution drafted. Have it ready by 3 P.M." He turned to me and reassured me, "I'll sign it and personally take it to the Monetary Board and the Department of Finance. We're having a meeting this afternoon."

Thus did Secretary Jose Concepcion of the Department of Trade and Industry remove the last barrier to the opening of our factory.

This experience

confirmed my belief that if you are without connection, it's so difficult to get things done quickly. But yet, it's so easy when they want to do it. Were it not for my persistence in getting the SGS exemption and commitment to the project's success, Sumida-Philippines would not have even started.

Also, the jobs it was to generate were very critical at that point in time because of the December 1989 coup that practically halted investments, both foreign and domestic, due to the unstable political and economic conditions of the Philippines. The attitude was one of wait-and-see and capital flight again took center stage. Hence, this opportunity of a coil and filter parts plant was too good not to be supported.

Secretary Concepcion saw the urgency of the situation and, to his credit, actively supported the solution to our SGS problem.

All production requirements were prepared in great frenzy and, finally, production operations started in January 1990. The trainees were back from China where they had been exposed to the actual production process of coils manufacture, plus the stringent quality control standards of Sumida-Far East.

Then the December Coup
took place.

The company was still installing new machineries and hiring new employees, when the dissident army group of Col. Gregorio Honasan (now Senator Honasan) launched their bloodiest coup attempt on December 1, 1989. It took two full weeks before they surrendered.

By chance, I left for Hong Kong the day before the December 1 coup d'etat to attend to some business matters. I proceeded to the Sumida plant in China to assure our trainees that the coup was taking place only in the Makati Commercial Center and was certainly not affecting the lives of their families and the rest of the country. I also wanted to encourage and inspire them to be hopeful and to trust in the good Lord who is their greatest Protector. I brought along lots of cookies, biscuits, and fruits for their *kasayahan* (delight). My trainees were all happy to see me come all the way to visit them in their workplace. I, too, was deeply gratified to see them well taken cared of in China.

When the coup happened, both Mr. Yawata and I were faced with the question of whether to continue the project or not. Eventually, we decided to push through with the project. We did not falter. On their return from China by Christmas of 1989, the trainees were allowed to vacation till the year's end.

By the end of January 1990, the company decided to start up one production line. It was an on-the-job training for our production employees — both those who trained in China and those who did not. Those who trained in China took the lead in orienting those who were not sent for training. It wasn't regular production yet. It was more of a dry-run operation.

It took all of six months for clear identification and delineation of work. There was continuous hiring and training during this period until we built up an employment base of 800 employees excluding about 300 more who were employed by our outside contractors.

By July 1990, the company decided to go full blast.

Coils are tiny

vital parts of consumer electronic products that determine video or audio clarity. We had to produce millions of such coils monthly based on firm orders from Sumida-Far East. Our production volume gradually built up but this was, of course, far from comparable to the production output of the China and Malaysia factories of Sumida since these factories had more time and more training.

Yet because of our desire to boost their morale, we would give the employees encouragement and inspire them to better their counterparts in other countries. Signs and slogans were put up all over the factory premises which said: "We aim to make Sumida (Philippines) the best Sumida plant in the world" or "We are quality people. We produce only the best."

All these were psychologically helpful in instilling high quality performance. So from a low production output, we gradually increased our production volume. There was a clear showing of Filipino productivity in our factory which was slowly building up as more production skills and experience were acquired by the entire organization. We were catching up with the Sumida companies that were ahead of us by four years at least.

This early performance of our employees delighted Sumida-Far East and made them confident of our operations. Our productivity chart clearly indicated the extent and adaptability of our people to excel.

Sumida-Far East was so happy

that they gave citations to our workers and the General Manager, who was seconded from Sumida-Far East, gave an outing/excursion to our workers to show their appreciation.

For the first quarter of 1992, Sumida-Philippines produced 18,035,000 coils which, if compared to China, were less. But we kept on encouraging our employees because we believed that given two years on the job, they would eventually prove superior.

The production process constituted the very heart of Sumida-Philippines. Since the company exported all its products overseas, it competed with the wholly-owned subsidiaries of Sumida-Far East operating in China, Taiwan, and Malaysia.

Cost and quality of our products became life and death issues for our company. We had to show that the cost and quality of Sumida-Philippines products were just as good if not better than those of the wholly-owned subsidiaries. It was a natural handicap — operating as an independent Filipino company.

Four main production lines

were eventually operated in Sumida-Philippines, namely: the RF line which made coils for radio transformers, the CD line which made coils for computer models, the IFT line which made coils for intermediate frequency transformers, and the Yobikako line which was essentially a sub-assembly line for the insertion of condensers in printed circuit boards (PCBs).

Each main production line could have one or more assembly lines so that at its peak, the company operated 23 assembly lines on two shifts. At least 14 people worked on each line headed by a line leader.

The line leader reported to a section leader who supervised a number of assembly lines. The section leader in turn reported directly to a production supervisor who was in charge of the entire production shift.

The two production supervisors reported to the General Manager who was a Hong Kong British national. He was also a manager in Sumida-Far East but was seconded to the Philippines. As GM, he was responsible for the production of the coils according to the order schedule. He held the concurrent positions of Production Manager, Quality

Assurance Manager, and Engineering Manager in the company. He had previous production management experience in other Sumida plants in China, South Africa and Canada. Another Hong Kong British national assisted the GM as Production Supervisor.

The company also had a Production Planning and Materials Control Department headed by a Japanese expatriate from Sumida-Far East who was relatively new to the Sumida organization having only recently transferred from another electronics firm.

A complement of Filipino supervisors and section leaders composed the front line management echelon of Sumida-Philippines. All of them, without exception, were part of the initial batch of engineers and technicians sent to China for training. They had come up through the ranks before obtaining their incumbent positions. Without exception, too, it was the first management experience for each of them.

By the end of June 1992,

the company had a total workforce of 853 people. Except for those who went to China for training, these people were with us for less than a year. Of the 90 who trained in China, one came home for fear of the coup, one was rushed home for kissing a Chinese lady worker which would have subjected him to an investigation and possible sanction if found guilty of violating Chinese factory rules, one changed her mind just before the scheduled departure, and one was dismissed upon arrival home for very poor performance in China.

The main bulk of our workforce was with the Production Department where there were 740 people.

Around 123 of these production people qualified

under the Department of Labor and Employment's (DOLE) apprenticeship program which the company availed itself of after obtaining the required DOLE approval.

The local head count for the other departments were: Finance and Personnel, 24; Production Engineering, 22; Quality Assurance, 34; Materials and Technical Support, 12; Production Planning and Materials Control, 21.

Just as I had anticipated, the business was labor-intensive. I was glad that we were providing jobs for our countrymen. The venture was also bringing foreign exhange revenues.

Towards the latter part of 1992, we hired a Deputy General Manager. He was Filipino yet fluent in both Japanese and Cantonese which was an asset in communicating with our expat managers.

By the time he joined our company, the GM from Hong Kong had already left to take a much needed vacation which eventually culminated in his resignation as he and his family migrated to Canada.

The newly hired Deputy GM was groomed to be the GM of the company after first going through an understudy period under the GM. However, at the time that the GM left, the Deputy GM had not yet assumed the GM position. Thus, Sumida-Philippines was run on concurrent basis by two expatriate engineers of Sumida-Far East. Mr. T. Oyo was especially brought in to improve Sumida-Philippines so that it could be at par with the other Sumida factories in Asia.

The employees decided

to form a union barely a year after the company started production operations in commercial quantity.

Just as an entrepreneur must anticipate problems

from without such as delays in getting government approvals and permits, he must likewise anticipate problems from within the company.

But for my faith in our workers who had been given the best of training and much better working conditions than some of them ever had experienced in the sweatshops where they used to work (especially the newly-hired ones), I would have seen the storm clouds gathering in the horizon.

Despite internal misgivings that it was not yet the right time for our employees to unionize, we did not prevent them from forming their union which was their right as guaranteed under the Philippine Constitution.

We were apprehensive though that the focus on work and productivity could be diverted to political union activities. At any rate, a union they wanted, so a union they got. We consoled ourselves with the thought that a responsible union could even be good for the company.

They filed the necessary documents with the DOLE and by March 6, 1992, the union was certified by a majority of Sumida-Philippines employees. They elected six officers. They called their union the Sumida Employees Union and it allied itself with a labor federation that was part of a national labor center (umbrella organization of various labor federations).

On April 15, 1992, the union submitted its collective bargaining agreement (CBA) proposal.

Then came the CBA meetings. The Deputy GM was assisted by the Personnel Manager during the negotiations with the union leaders in what seemed to be never-ending meetings.

The union demands
were non-negotiable and included, among many other unreasonable conditions, an across the board wage increase

of P25.00 per day in addition to existing benefits like free uniforms and subsidized meals.

It should be pointed out that the company's hiring rate for regular employees is at least equal to the mandated minimum wage and employees are paid overtime and night differential pay as are appropriate and in accordance with existing labor laws. Negotiations went on from April until August 1992 without any let-up. As we correctly predicted, the company's energies were shifted from work to union activities. Output suffered. Our personnel manager was on the family way and got physically exhausted with every CBA meeting.

Sabotage occurred.

During the time that the CBA negotiations were underway, Sumida-Far East informed us that a shipment from Sumida-Philippines of one-million coils to their South African customer was totally rejected because it was found that these coils were filled with epoxy that made them totally unusable. This was the start of sabotage work being done by the labor union. Afterwards, rejections increased.

We were having more than the average "lots out" as these rejections were called. For the most part, the rejections were not raw materials defect but were clearly production defects which were intentionally done by the operators.

Consider this case: Part of the production process included packing the finished coils into boxes which were then sealed and placed inside shipping cartons. These boxes were so designed to hold an exact number of coils to expedite their inventory. The loss of even one small coil could be noticed easily. Our customers began receiving an alarming number of boxes with missing coils, thus disrupting the inventory process and causing delays in their production due to parts shortages.

The one-million coils that were filled with epoxy were sabotaged in the quality assurance section which was in the hands of the union leaders. We tried to rework the damaged coils but the process was so tedious and the recovery was so marginal that we were forced to destroy them.

As a result of the sabotage, business was driven away from us and we were subjected to penalties for delayed deliveries.

We were to learn later that these damaged coils were to be supplied to Sony for their camera-recorders (handy-cam). We stepped up the production of these coils to cover for the damaged quantity under strict supervision, but in the end Sumida-Far East had to supply part of the quantity ordered from their other Sumida factories.

It was really sad to see the havoc that misguided union leaders could bring. Because the CBA negotiations were going nowhere, I personally appealed to three groups of employees: the managers and supervisors, the line leaders, and the line workers and other rank and file employees. I practically told them the same thing.

"Let us not destroy

what we have started. Think of tomorrow when we will all reap many good benefits.

"I have great dreams for this company. We can be better than all the other Sumida plants in Asia. We can be number one in production and productivity. I know this can be done. I strongly believe that given the breaks,

Filipinos will prove to be efficient, competent, and render far superior service.

"Let's prove first that we can do it. Why ask for a wage increase when we have just started? Many of you have wages far above those you used to receive after backbreaking long hours of work under substandard working conditions. I know this because you intimated these to me during your job interviews, remember?

"Here, you have a good working environment. Air-conditioned. Lots of space so that you don't feel suffocated. A nice cafeteria. You are sufficiently guided by experts who so unselfishly share their expertise with you. You are working for a company whose heart reaches out to you and anticipates your needs even before you ask for them. Don't you believe me?" I pleaded passionately despite some audible heckling from some union officers.

"Don't you trust me?"

I begged them again and again to consider their families. "You are now learning new skills, meeting new friends. You are no longer a liability but an asset to yourselves, your family, and our country."

I could sense that my sincerity was winning them over and I became hopeful. There were some sectors, mostly the active union leaders and their close followers, who maintained that I was just acting and that I deserved an acting award for my performance.

But I kept my faith.

I knew deep inside my heart that enlightenment would come to them and would prove me right. I knew that in time they would see how strong my concern was for them and the welfare of their families.

Sumida-Far East officials met

with me to express their concern over the impending strike that could worsen the already deteriorating quality of Sumida-Philippines products and wreak more havoc on delivery schedules.

"Our customers are industrial manufacturers who can't afford to wait for your labor problems to be threshed out," they stressed. "If you cannot assure us that the strike will not happen, we will be forced to give in to our customers' requests to shift their supply source to Sumida-China."

"It is beyond our control," I honestly told them. "I can't guarantee that there'll be no strike. It's all up to the union, but I'll continue appealing to them so that a strike may be averted."

I appealed again to the union leaders and workers to consider their position. I asked them to finish the coils to be ready for shipment by November 1. I told them that if we were unable to produce the quantity of coils ordered, Sumida-Far East would not ship the raw materials and there would be no work by October.

But my appeal fell on deaf ears. The union leaders did not believe me. I later on learned that they thought I was bluffing and my appealing to them was just an act.

In the light of the union leaders' stubborn stand, I went to the factory to appeal to the good sense of the workers and for them not to listen to those who would destroy us. I told them to exercise their own judgment and not be just mere followers. I asked them to reconsider my appeal to commit themselves to produce the coils that were needed to be shipped in November.

The workers were divided. I thought that many

believed in what I told them. I hoped that those who believed would be able to convince their fellow workers and influence their union leaders.

My recourse had been to appeal

to their good sense. But instead of considering my appeal, under the guidance or misguidance of their union leaders, the workers stepped up their communications campaign against the company that was their bread and butter.

The union leaders had been very active in putting up exhortative posters and letters on company bulletin boards which made significant impact on our employees. They really believed that we were not an independent company but that we were part of a large multinational group — the Sumida Group — and that they could get what they wanted because of the huge investments that were plowed into the project.

That the union leaders were able to sell this erroneous information to majority of our workers showed that we were not very effective in our information campaign even though all the company managers and supervisors did their best in explaining the company status to their people and the consequences of their threat to go on strike.

We had what seemed to be an impasse in the CBA negotiations.

Then came

a request from the union leaders for me to meet the executive of their labor center.

I immediately acceded to the request, hopeful that with the right understanding and leadership of a more mature labor executive, the impasse could be bridged. We met at a place of their choice in Roxas Boulevard, Manila. Present were the union leaders, their lawyer, and the labor center's executive.

"I think that this is a good meeting. I'm happy to meet a high ranking labor center official as well as the union's lawyer so we can thresh out our present problem in Sumida-Philippines," I started. "As I've said in my talks to my employees, I have their welfare at heart. Precisely, no stone was left unturned to make Sumida-Philippines survive under a very trying time.

"When I started this project in 1989, I had great hopes for the success of this company. At that time, the semi-conductor and allied industries were on the rise due to the expected economic improvement of the country. But, alas! The recession in the U.S., Europe and Japan has deepened and worsened. Factories are being closed, layoffs by the hundreds of thousands are taking place in these countries, many once well-established companies like Macy's, Sears, Bullocks, have become bankrupt. Philips of Netherlands has announced it will be laying off 45,000 employees in the next few years, the car companies are suffering in all countries.

"All these are signs of the bad times that we are in and we should not hurt our present position when we are just starting and most of our employees are under one year employment.

"We are still learning new skills and our engineers are still undergoing training in Japan. All these will go to waste if you insist on your union demands. Most of our employees are new hires and for many of them this is their first job. Others have transferred to us from sweatshops and factories that hired them on piece-rate basis. Surely, they can compare how good we have been treating them.

"There should be pride and honor in their hearts that they are working for a Filipino company and yet are getting international skills needed for the export of their production.

"Let us not destroy ourselves and, worst, our country. Our company is dependent on the goodwill, trust, and confidence of our foreign buyer who also supplies us with both raw materials and technology to do the job.

"Why don't we continue our good relationship and redeem ourselves from the already bad image we have now with our buyers by our irresponsible acts in the past few months by causing damage to over one million pieces of coils, lacking parts and erroneous quantities in the boxes shipped out, and the slowdown in work you have been exhibiting this past couple of months.

"All is not lost. We can still get into the good graces of our buyer but we have to work sincerely together and to think of the future instead of your insistent demand for a CBA with its unreasonable conditions.

"Look, why don't we just have a one year moratorium and after which we can talk again. Maybe, by that time the world recession would have been eased out and the business will become buoyant again. Let's conserve our goodwill and work to the best of our abilities so that we can be in a better position to talk about your demands.

"I have presented our financial statements and income tax returns to you which show very clearly that we are in the red. How can we immediately get profits when it is common knowledge that for a manufacturing company, the first three years are the hardest and preparatory years because of the capital requirements and the training time needed to get the expected quality and quantity output.

We're just hardly into the second year of our actual manufacturing operations and already we do not belong to the same team."

I must have made a good half-hour hard talk to bring the picture to them.

I was floored

by the reply of the labor center's executive. "Why don't you just give them P25.00 per day across the board increase and everything will be solved?"

"I don't think you heard what I said. It's not a question of giving the money. The issue here is the life of the company. Even at the present condition, the company is losing money. We are willing to invest, but this act of filing a notice to strike and having the sword hanging on the company will bring ruin to us all. The buyer will not send us their raw materials for production if there is a threat of not being able to deliver to them the finished parts. It's a matter of life and death for all of us," I answered.

I was surprised to hear the union lawyer make his comment at this point. He said, "Mrs. Lim is giving us a good solution. Why don't we consider a one year moratorium and bring up the discussion after?"

His comment did not find favor with the union officers and the labor center executive. They insisted on their demand.

The meeting lasted for almost two hours to no avail.

I left asking them to consider everything I had said. I challenged them to validate the financial statements of the company which I gave them. I begged them not to be reckless, not to destroy what we had worked so hard for, not to waste everything we had accomplished together.

"Think of what injury you will cause if we don't settle this. Our buyer is waiting for the outcome of this meeting. They have already mentioned the difficult business environment taking place and that even their own factories, including those in China and Malaysia, are crying out for more orders. They also have hopes of a good Philippine manufacturing base, that is why they're supporting us.

"If you can't give a written assurance that the raw materials for October-November production will be done and shipped out safely, they will be constrained to shift these raw materials to their other factories. The consequence of a delayed delivery is additional cost and loss of business. They will be subjected to penalties by their respective buyers if they fail to deliver these parts."

I left the meeting very deeply hurt and disillusioned. It saddened me that despite all the good things we had in such a short time, the irresponsibility of a few union leaders and their advisers could drive them into suicidal action.

The end came

on August 20, 1992, when we received a fax message from Sumida-Far East informing us that they would no longer be ordering from Sumida-Philippines for the following reasons:

1. The worldwide recession which was affecting their coil business tremendously as demand for coils dropped in 1992 by about 35%. As a result, there was very strong competition among coil producers in the reduced market.

2. Their present customers would not accept coil reduction from the Philippines due to the experience of high rejection. Also, the Notice to Strike filed by the labor union of Sumida-Philippines would cause them great damage if the coils would not be delivered on time.

3. They understood our strong appeal for continued orders for

Sumida-Philippines and even hid from their customers the problems of Sumida-Philippines, but still their customers insisted on getting their coils from other sources except Sumida-Philippines, otherwise these customers would stop buying from Sumida-Far East and would change suppliers for their coil requirements.

4. Accordingly, they had no more orders for Sumida-Philippines to produce for the September-October 1992 production. The orders of their present customers were shifted to their China factory so as not to lose these customers to competitors.

5. They were still paying for the cost of claims of customers which were served by production coming from Sumida-Philippines. They could no longer afford to take any further risks.

We were informed that they would try to get new orders from other customers so that Sumida-Philippines could continue its operations. However, we knew that the business was up for hard times with no customer already willing to take a risk with Sumida-Philippines.

My son, Vincent S. Lim, who was VP-Finance of Sumida-Philippines, tried to convince Sumida-Far East to reconsider the Philippines as a steady source of finished coils. Unfortunately, his appeal was also not acted on favorably by Sumida-Far East.

I called for a general assembly

of all employees of Sumida-Philippines and I told them about the situation concerning the company's business. I also told them of the decision of our lone customer, Sumida-Far East.

There was no recourse for us but to file with the Department of Labor and Employment (DOLE) a notice to lay off our employees starting September 3, 1992, but we were still hoping for a turn of events — that the market would recover and that Sumida-Far East would change their mind about the Philippines. It was this hope that prevented us from filing our company's Notice of Closure.

On November 10, 1992, however, we received the following faxed message from Sumida-Far East: "*We regret to inform you that due to very poor prospect of regaining customers' orders for Sumida (Phil.) production in both near and long term, we have come to the final conclusion that there can be no more orders to Sumida (Phil.) in the future.*

"*We appreciate your efforts to get orders from Sumida (FE) so that your workers will continue to have work. However, the reduced market due to economic recession and stiffer competition we are facing for cost, price and quality efficiency has left us no other recourse but to stop orders from you.*

"*We hope you will understand our position and business decision.*"

This was the message that we were afraid of receiving from Sumida-Far East.

We had tried our best to protect the interest of our employees, but it was clear to us that the uncooperative stance of the employees' labor union was actually the last straw that broke the proverbial camel's back. Sumida-Far East did not want to have anything to do with us anymore because of our labor problem.

When all else failed,

we filed our Notice of Closure of Sumida-Philippines with the DOLE. At the same time, we notified our employees of this decision.

By this time, they realized they had made a big mistake. Many were blaming each other and some wanted to beat the daylights out of their union president who absented himself lest he fall into the hands of the irate union members.

Some employees, especially the rank-and-file clerical and support staff, were willing to work for P80.00 daily wage which was much lower than the P128.00 minimum daily wage plus overtime pay and many other fringe benefits they were getting. They were so immature they didn't get the point. They thought it was a matter of pay. They forgot that they had jeopardized everything by blindly following their union leaders. By doing so, the solidarity between management and employees was broken. A divided house cannot stand.

Poetry has

often been a great source of help and comfort for me, especially during very difficult times, when things are beyond words, when problems defy conventional management solutions.

One poem, written three centuries ago, speaks to us from the ages.

KNOW THEN THYSELF

Know then thyself, presume not God to scan,
The proper study of mankind is Man.
Placed on this isthmus of a middle state,
A being darkly wise and rudely great:
With too much knowledge for the Sceptic side,
With too much weakness for the Stoic's pride,

He hangs between; in doubt to act or rest,
In doubt to deem himself a God or Beast,
In doubt his mind or body to prefer;
But born to die, and reasoning but to err;
Alike in ignorance, his reason such
Whether he thinks too little or too much:
Chaos of thought and passion, all confused;
Still by himself abused, or disabused;
Created half to rise and half to fall;
Great lord of all things, yet a prey to all;
Sole judge of truth, in endless error hurled;
The glory, jest, and riddle of the world!
Go, wondrous creature! mount where science guides:
Go, measure earth, weigh air, and state the tides:
Instruct the planets in what orbs to run,
Correct old time and regulate the Sun;
Go, soar with Plato to th' empyreal sphere,
To the first good, first perfect, and first fair;
Or tread the mazy round his follow'rs trod
And quitting sense call imitating God -
As Eastern priests in giddy circles run,
And turn their heads to imitate the Sun.
Go, teach Eternal Wisdom how to rule:
Then drop into thyself, and be a fool!
Superior beings, when of late they saw
A mortal man unfold all natures's law,
Admired such wisdom in an earthly shape,
And showed a Newton as we show an ape.
Could he, whose rules the rapid comet bind,
Describe or fix one movement of his mind?
Who saw its fires here rise and there descend,
Explain his own beginning or his end?
Alas, what wonder: man's superior part

Unchecked may rise, and climb from art to art,
But when his own great work is but begun,
What reason weaves by passion is undone.

— *from "An Essay on Man"*
by Alexander Pope
1688-1744

These lines describe the character and nature of human beings. "With too much weakness for the Stoic's pride" and imbued with deep passion that can easily end all good things without reason.

In the end, we lost

our customer, we lost our jobs, we lost everything.

I remember how, in a final effort to avert the terrible consequences of a strike, I made one final pitch to our employees.

"We're just newly born. We can still look forward to many years of growth and sustainable development. Let's not lose this chance. Each of us has a role in nation-building. Let us understand this role and do our work with unity and excellence. Anything less will destroy us."

Sadly, we missed our chance. We missed a golden opportunity to be an active participant in national development in this particular manufacturing activity. Along with the loss of our jobs, we also lost our yet to be learned skills and knowledge, and many more benefits for our family and country. A painful lesson indeed.

Today, Sumida-China has 6,000 workers; Malaysia, 4,000 workers. Philippines: ZERO.

The Sumida Experience

brought several fundamental questions to my mind.

Is it right to leave the workers' security in the hands of unscrupulous union leaders?

How should we educate the workers to discern between caring and uncaring union leaders?

Who has a greater stake in the welfare of the employees?

What started as a great promise ended up in shattered dreams and broken, unmendable pieces of wasted opportunities.

Everything is now moot and academic. The workers closed Sumida-Philippines. My conscience is clear. I did all I could to avert the disastrous end, but the union members decided to stand united. And united, they fell.

We are answerable

for our actions. God gave us the freedom to choose. This is the only freedom that is absolutely innate to a human being.

I cry not so much for my loss, but the greater loss of others — people and country.

Whose hand was it that moved the weak hearts and minds to create such a waste?

What lessons are we to learn from this coiled experience?

Chapter Seven

Agri-Business and Countryside Development

REAPING BY SOWING

In my heart,
there has always been a special place for the *barrio*, the small farming and fishing villages that make up the Philippine countryside.

Thus, among the accomplishments of the Solid Group of Companies (SGC), we are particularly proud that long before "countryside development" became the buzzword in government and business circles, SGC was already deep into agriculture and aqua-culture.

I guess my heartfelt concern for countryside development stems from my rural roots. I grew up in Leyte, a remote and impoverished Philippine province.

Leyte's first and probably only real claim to world history is that it was the landing point of General Douglas MacArthur in the U.S. liberation of the Philippines from Japanese occupation during World War II. The landing occurred on October 20, 1944. This signaled the death toll to the Japanese imperial ambition to create a Greater East Asia Co-Prosperity Sphere under its influence if not domination.

As a young girl

growing up in Tacloban, then the capital town of Leyte Province, I had my first encounter with countryside business when our family planted corn at the backyard of our leased property

This was during the Japanese occupation years when food was scarce and life was trying and dangerous. To augment our food supply, all of us (my mother and six children) planted corn in an empty lot, measuring approximately 1,000 square meters, behind our house.

This was my first experience to use simple hand tools to loosen the soil. We worked before daybreak and in between work and studies at home and school, would zealously clear the area of debris, weeds, garbage, stones and oftentimes would not stop until the last ray of sunlight had turned day into night.

After many backbreaking hours,

we finally succeeded in seeding the area. For several months, our family took turns in nursing the young corn until they were ripe for harvest.

However, at harvest time, we found many Japanese soldiers already harvesting the corn. Timidly, we asked if we could pluck some corn, too. In fairness to the young Japanese men, they did allow us to get a basketful. This was already considered just and fair because they could have completely denied our request.

One must understand the environment at that time. There was a vicious war going on. The Filipino guerillas were active in our province and there were daily encounters between the two forces and casualties mounting on both sides did not exactly breed benevolent hearts. War is evil. People suffer. Food is scarce. Survival was the rule. It doesn't take much imagination to understand how enmity and injustice can become the normal conduct.

We got our portion of the corn which we shared with our neighbors. This was the best that could happen. It was enough for us to continue on planting for the next harvest season. The cycle was similarly repeated. We planted and the harvest was shared by many. But I learned how to plant and harvest corn. I call this my first experience in agriculture. Isn't it wonderful to learn this art under a difficult time?

During those days,

there was also this woman farmer who would bring into town two or three baskets of tomatoes from her small farm in Catarman, Samar. Samar being an even poorer province than Leyte, she would bring tomatoes to our shoe store in Tacloban and sell her tomatoes to us.

Mother would buy her tomatoes and resell them along the sidewalk of the wet market in retail. As far as I can recollect, it was sold for five to six pieces for a few centavos. I was assigned this task. I would neatly cluster the tomatoes on the sidewalk on an old paper and before long, the tomatoes would all be sold.

The quantities were small — two or three baskets— and this experience took place everytime the woman farmer brought her tomatoes to Tacloban. Of course, this was not a daily chore. It depended on the availability of the tomatoes.

As a young girl, I learned the art of sidewalk micro-retail selling thru the tomato route. It made me stronger in the sense that I learned to relate to people. It taught me patience and humility. It taught me to have a pleasant disposition, to greet and smile at customers. Perhaps this explains why smiling comes easily and naturally to me. It

must have been honed somehow during my first stint at business
— selling tomatoes.

I also learned

the art of reading and translating comic books to my customers
who were mostly the poor children of Tacloban.

This was part of my countryside business during the
war years. Due to the absence of books, papers and magazines,
I picked up the old discarded comic books of a rich classmate
and hung them along the wall of our store. I rented out the
comic books for a few centavos. This brought in many customers,
both old and young, all eager and hungry for reading materials.

This experience was to be enhanced with translating
the comic stories into the Visayan dialect to the delight of the
children. The reading and translating experience turned me
from a very shy girl to a more outgoing and sociable adolescent.
I made friends. I learned to smile and laugh more. I laughed
with the characters of the comic books. I was earning and
enjoying at the same time.

My entrepreneurial widowed mother

spruced up the little store with fried peanuts. So, aside from
renting out comic books, we also had fried peanuts to boot.
This business was mine and my elder sister, Teresa, to do. We
must have done a pretty good job because this lasted almost to
the end of the war years. The comic books were read again
and again, translated and retranslated as there were no new
ones coming anymore. It was the same original discarded set
of maybe less than a hundred pieces. But it was enough to last
through the war years.

The main business of my mother was making shoes
and slippers. On the earnings of a shoemaker, plus small
side businesses like comic books, tomatoes, and peanuts,

we survived.

I have narrated these incidents to show

that agribusiness and countryside business can be found in every nook and cranny in the Philippines.

This kind of experience is shared today by hundreds of thousands of micro-entrepreneurs. My business was indeed "micro-micro." I did not then envision that someday I would be very involved in the areas of activities I now find myself in. How was I to know what God would want me to do for Him?

Such as our involvement in the shrimp

industry which now covers hatchery operations and aquaculture in ponds found in Panay and Zamboanga; processing plants in strategic centers such as Manila, Roxas City (Capiz province), Bacolod (Negros Occidental), Ozamiz City (Misamis Oriental Province), Tacloban (Leyte Province), Ipil La Paz (Zamboanga del Sur). All our produce are exported to Japan, U.S., Canada, Hawaii, Guam, Hongkong and South Korea.

Milkfish production

is another major project in the countryside.

Only a couple of years ago, we purchased a poorly developed milkfish pond in a small impoverished town called Numancia which to me sounds like "No Man's Land." We developed the pond into a more productive one. We built the first and only ice plant in the town.

Until our arrival in Numancia, Aklan Province, there used to be some traders who purchased the produce of the small aqua milkfish farmers at a price much lower than that of the more prosperous towns, Numancia being far from the port and the roads bad.

After we established our ice plant and processing plant, we put up a price at par with the progressive towns, approximately 10 to 20% higher. Sadly, we put the old traders out of business. The local farmers now knew where to bring their produce. We pay higher prices because of the presence of an ice plant and storage facilities. We are doing a good countryside business on milkfish in Numancia, Aklan Province, and in Roxas, Capiz Province.

This story is repeated in the other provinces where we have our buying stations, grow out ponds, processing and packaging plants which all serve the communities wherever they are situated. All these plants have ice plant and storage facilities.

A very interesting experience

is the purchase of a grow-out pond operations and processing plant in Zamboanga which was owned by one of the top bankers in the country. It is a huge operation and perhaps a quarter of a billion pesos was sunk into its operations. After so many years, the losses continue to mount until one day the banker called it quits.

After a brief negotiation, we bought the plant. It was our desire to bring it back to life after it was closed for some time. We are now refurbishing the plant and rebuilding the ponds. We will hire people and train them after completion of the renovation.

Today, we are breathing new life to this plant. Commercial production has not started because we are still in the process of making more improvements. We have hired a French consulting firm to audit the plant and its production process. We have high expectations from this investment. Indeed, a great promise awaits. The community will be served and I hope to be a part of the historical growth of this shrimp industry in this region. As the old saying goes, "While others let go, new ones will carry the torch and hold it even higher." This is my experience in a town called Ipil La Paz in the province of Zamboanga del Sur.

We have also

put up a facility in Barangay Ipil (outside of Ormoc City), Leyte, which produces alcohol from molasses. It employs a good number of local residents. Equally important is our impact on the tax revenues of the province. We are now the largest taxpayer in Leyte.

In addition, we have contributed computer sets to the Ipil Public High School, the barangay council, and the City Disaster Coordinating Council of Ormoc City.

Further, we provide an Annual AA Scholarship Award for the local high school's valedictorian. The scholarship covers the entire college course at the Visayas State College of Agriculture, the No.1 root crop research center in the Philippines, if not in Asia.

Our General Manager, Mr. Louie Zabaljauregui, is also the volunteer adviser of the Department of Agriculture's Livelihood Enhancement and Agriculture Development (LEAD) Program. The volunteer work he is doing is an example of how we are sharing our technical and management expertise to improve the lives of our fellow-Filipinos in the countryside.

The Management Association

of the Philippines (MAP) is the biggest and most prestigious management organization in the country.

As a governor of the MAP board and chairperson of its Agribusiness and Countryside Development Committee, I chair the committee's weekly Tuesday meeting (from 7 to 9 A.M.). It is such a pleasure to work with the committee members. They are all senior leaders in their own right, active and truly committed to social service and to promoting agribusiness and countryside development.

Our committee assists government agencies in the study, discussion and even formulation of policies· for the country's food security programs. We act as volunteer advisers to various coops in 25 provinces in implementing government programs to deliver training services to farmers in rural areas.

This is one activity I perform with deep satisfaction. Waking up every Tuesday morning at the break of dawn to chair this Committee's meeting of learned men and women in agriculture is a wonderful and fulfilling learning experience for me. I count this as one of the delightful blessings in my life.

Countryside development through electronics

has also proven to be a viable strategy. As the exclusive manufacturer and distributor of Sony electronic products in the Philippines for the past 25 years, I have made a policy of product and service dispersal quite opposite to what my competitors have done. Instead of transferring the responsibility of service to third parties or independent repair shops, I have made it my responsibilty, since our early days, to assure quality servicing available to all our nationwide customers through our own service network.

The decision to take on this responsibility was not an easy one to make, especially with the problem of logistics that we had to contend with. Another problem in the first 10 years of our corporate life was that there were more Sony products that were in the market through the backdoor than from our factory.

This was quite easy to ascertain through our service network. All the goods sourced from us had serial numbers in every unit for us to give our service warranties. Through the service data, we discovered that we did about 60% servicing on units that did not come from our factory, easily translatable to units brought into the country either through the backdoor or simply handcarried by passengers via airports through their travels.

Of course, there was also servicing rendered to those given exemptions on their household or office goods such as members of the diplomatic corps or government agencies. But this was a very small number compared to the rest. By serial number we discovered that about 80 to 90% of those serviced outside of our domestic sales came from Hong Kong. This seemed natural because Hong Kong is a free port and goods sold there are tax-free; it is also very near, being only an hour and a half flight from Manila.

Fortunately, the situation has improved over the years. The reduction of tariff walls on electronic finished products from 100% to today's 30% has made smuggling a diminishing problem for legitimate manufacturers. The reduction of tariffs for parts from 30% to 10% has also greatly enhanced the competitiveness of local manufacturers.

I remember how,

during our early days, some of our managers suggested that we turn away units not purchased from our source as a policy to deter smuggling. This looked like too simplistic a solution. Pricewise, we also couldn't compete because Sony products bought in Hong Kong were easily 40 to 50% cheaper than their Philippine counterparts because of the high local tax.

One way of competing could have been through the service network. Denying them the warranties of genuine parts and quality service would perhaps have deterred them from bringing in Sony products from abroad. But as I told my managers then: "It will not be a good image for us because a Sony product should assure quality at all times. Quality means not only the product but on the continued use and enjoyment of the product. Denying parts and good service at a time when a customer needs it would reflect on the image of Sony and may adversely affect their good name."

I remember my sales manager arguing, "But ma'am, we will be carrying a heavier load of parts inventory because the units brought in from abroad are of many models and we only manufacture specific models. How can we, for example, carry on stock picture tubes of different sizes when we are only making Sony television of three sizes, 12 inches, 14 inches, and 20 inches? This is not to mention the many internal parts which differ according to their models. We will be training and hiring more engineers and technicians to do their repair, plus we have to do house servicing when requested by customers."

No doubt my manager's apprehension had merits. He further noted: "Look at the other brands. None of them do direct servicing nationwide. Not only that. They refuse to service their own brands on units not coming from them. So they limit their parts inventory and logistics."

My sales manager had made his point

quite clear. However, I had to relate my decision to the long-term vision. That vision called for building the Sony name in the Philippines as the most reliable brand, both in product and in servicing.

Considering that Sony products came in ten years later than the other manufacturers who were here in the late sixties and early seventies, I believed then that the right decision was to keep on enhancing Sony's image through its service network.

Thus, we decided to accept all Sony units for service, store up as much common parts needed for service, and establish as many service centers as our logistics would allow.

To date, this decision has proved to be correct. We have established 28 Sony service centers throughout the country and most of them are in the countryside. Every year, we continue to develop at least one or two more service centers. This has made us the only electronics manufacturer in the Philippines with a vast network of countryside service centers with the mission of giving post-sales service at its best. It has also enabled us to make a significant contribution to the creation of employment opportunities in the countryside: Our service centers now employ hundreds of highly trained technicians, and even more will be employed in the future as we expand.

I remember an almost comical problem

which we encountered. We were losing our technicians as fast as we were training them. They left for abroad to seek jobs in the Middle East, then a haven for Filipino migrant workers.

We became a very good source of trained technicians who, after three to five years of work experience with us, were pirated by employment agencies or companies for jobs in countries with few skilled technicians or managers but with great development plans and programs, especially the Middle East.

At one time, it turned out to be a comical situation because we discovered that a Sony manager from the Middle East hired an employment recruiting firm in Manila to recruit Filipino technicians for Sony Middle East needs. This recruiting firm offered better pay and practically zeroed in his recruitment mission on our Sony-trained technicians who best fitted the jobs because of the training and experience they had from us.

When I discovered this, I wrote a letter to Sony and complained about this odd situation. A compromise was reached. Instead of Sony Middle East getting our technicians through a local employment agency, they furnished us in advance their required number of technicians and we chose them from our workforce. It was as an incentive for the latter to work in Sony M.E. at a salary we agreed upon with Sony.

We made sure this was higher than what the local employment agency gave (since the agency was earning a fat commission aside from the extraneous fees for the processing of the papers, etc.) with better benefits for a period of two years. At the end of the period, the technicians were to return to our outfit. This seemed a win-win situation for all. Our technicians got better pay abroad, Sony M.E. got the skilled technicians, and we got them back after two years. This also allowed a bigger number to work in Sony Middle East and certainly gave them an opportunity to earn and save.

I find it rather amusing that our company would have employees dispersed farther than the Philippine countryside. They went as far as the countryside of the Middle East countries. This surely went beyond my vision.

In the Philippines, service centers are found in almost all major cities and provinces. This has resulted in employing a huge complement of workforce attending to both sales and service activities.

Countryside development through exports
has been another highly effective strategy. Through the

Philippine Exporters Foundation (Philexport) of which I am a founding member, as well as President from 1986 to 1992, many Filipino exporters — most of whom are in the countryside — have been able to successfully lobby for the proper government support.

This has borne fruit as proven by the dramatic increase in Philippine export earnings, which has been growing since 1986. Philippine exports in 1995 reached about US $10 billion.

Philexport was originally conceived as a think-tank to help government boost exports through strategic plans. I transformed it into an umbrella organization of all Filipino exporters where they could speak through a single voice. It became a broadly based organization of exporters with professional executives and a board of reputable, competent individuals, imbued with a deep sense of integrity and service as they served without any compensation.

When I inherited the job of running Philexport in 1986, shortly after the new government of President Corazon Aquino was in place, it was in the red. There were no projects as it was doomed to obscurity as most well-intentioned foundations become when there are no funds to support it. I introduced the business arm by providing bonded warehouse service for a nominal fee to small and medium exporters who needed a common bonded warehouse to house the raw materials, parts, and equipment they imported for their exports.

At that time a bonded warehouse was not accessible because it needed the endorsement of the Secretary of Trade and Industry concurred in by the Chairman of the BOI. This endorsement was very difficult to get because of the apprehension of the Trade Secretary of the abuses allegedly or reportedly committed by some bonded warehouses who, instead of exporting their products, managed to sell their imported inputs to the domestic market tax-free and thus caused unfair competition to others.

Eventually, he endorsed the common bonded warehouse operation to the Bureau of Customs. This led to the business service made available to small and medium exporters. In support of this innovation, we were able to work out a US$8.7 million grant from USAID for information build-up. All these helped in the development of Philexport's services. I was able to do this only because of the support of a very high-powered, reputable, and credible board. Among them were Messrs. Francis Laurel, Art Sanvictores, Ramon Davila, Ricardo Gloria, Raul Boncan, and Tony Lo.

A common thread

running through all the diverse business projects of the Solid Group of Companies is the significant, long-term, and positive impact that they have on countryside development.

Through the series of industrial estate development projects we are undertaking which started with the Laguna International Industrial Park (LIIP), we are helping attract large foreign investments that, in turn, create thousands of new jobs and business opportunities in the provinces.

Our determined drive to make the black tiger prawn a billion-dollar export product for the Philippines will undoubtedly redound to the benefit of thousands of Filipino fisherfolk.

Our continuing commitment to provide Filipinos with a truly affordable and high-quality "People's Car" provides them with the mobility they need to speed up business growth in both urban and rural areas.

Projects in the electronics industry such as Kita Corporation in Clark are helping a lahar-devastated people literally rise from the ashes.

Sony, our flagship brand in electronics, will continue to bring not only greater employment as we expand operations but also the high technology we need to be fully competitive in the 21st century.

And so on, until our dream of a Philippine countryside throbbing with entrepreneurial activities, bursting with prosperity, will come true

Chapter Eight

Kita Corporation

A LEAP
OF FAITH

*...seeing the light through the
cloud of dust, clearly...*

I must have sounded crazy
to my executives and foreign business partners from Aiwa
then.

There I was, insisting on building a manufacturing
plant for Aiwa color TV — worth millions of dollars — in
the middle of an area totally devastated by the volcanic
fury of Mt. Pinatubo.

Everywhere you looked, you saw kilometers and
kilometers of grey, powdery lahar that came from the bowels
of Mt. Pinatubo, simmering for centuries until the explosion,
and now so deep that it submerged entire buildings and
made entire towns and landmarks disappear.

The place was so far from the world-class urban
comforts of Metro Manila. There was no road, no power, no
water, no phones, no nothing.

Just lahar and my fellow-Filipinos, destroyed in everything but their spirit, their determination to rebuild their lives.

What made my insistence
more incomprehensible to my colleagues was the fact that a far better alternative site — a million times better! — was there on a silver platter. The alternative was the newly opened Laguna International Industrial Park (LIIP) which we owned in partnership with Samsung Corporation of Korea.

LIIP had all the world-class infrastructure that investors need, and was so near Metro Manila! Comparing it with the lahar-filled area was like comparing gold with, well, lahar.

It all began
in 1993, at the opening of our Aiwa Showroom along T.M. Kalaw Street, Manila.

One of our guests was Mr. Hajime Unoki, President of Aiwa Co., Ltd., who had also been Sony's Chief of International Marketing. Making light conversation over cocktails, he told me that he hoped we would repeat for Aiwa what we did for Sony: Make Aiwa a household word. Not one to let opportunity pass, and knowing that Aiwa Japan was expanding in Malaysia and Singapore, I broached the concept of Aiwa manufacturing audio products in the Philippine.

After cocktails, we held a press conference and a reporter asked me to reveal what Aiwa will do next. I said that we were trying to convince Aiwa to invest in the Philippines by transferring their manufacturing operations here, similar to what they have done in Malaysia. It would bring employment to our people as well as generate revenue for our government.

When asked if Aiwa and Sony are the same, Mr. Unoki clarified that Aiwa is a subsidiary of Sony.

"What plans do you have for the Philippines? Are you investing with Mrs. Lim?" the reporter asked.

Mr. Unoki replied that he would like to study the investment possibility here. To do this, he would need detailed preparations and research on the Philippine advantages.

He added that Aiwa has invested in Malaysia because it has all the good factors in place, such as infrastructure, power, telephones, transportation, and the like. Labor costs and government regulations are transparent, clear, and efficient. Tariffs and taxes are low, hence, many component suppliers are there; people are religious and honest; employees are hardworking and eager to learn. Entry and exit of goods and raw materials, so he said, are automatic because of the good customs system. Besides, emphasized Mr. Unoki, neighboring markets are within convenient reach.

"I think the Philippines has its good points. I have known Mrs. Lim many long years in my Sony days," Mr. Unoki told the reporter, "and her family is also our distributor of Aiwa here in the Philippines, so we will study together what's best."

It turned out after a year, that the best was for our family to invest in the production of Aiwa products for export to Japan, the Middle East, the European Community and the U.S.

Aiwa did not want to invest in factories (machines and buildings) because their new strategy called for others to invest in Aiwa products. They would, however, assist in technical and logistic development, as well as assure global market.

Even with this strategy, Aiwa is very choosy in the selection of its production partner. Our relationship with Sony as its exclusive manufacturer in the Philippines since 1971 up to the present provided an exemplary track record that made Aiwa immediately choose us for its production partner.

The next question
was what to call the new company.

After studying many options, we decided on "Kita Corporation."

The word "Kita" stands for several positive meanings by simply changing one's accent or stress when enunciating it.

In Japanese, Kita refers to the North, a cardinal point in the compass, which is a direction pointing to the right of a person when facing the setting sun. Pronounced another way, it also means "much abundance."

In architecture, north is the only direction marked on plans which is enough to indicate where the other directions (east, west, and south) lie.

In various Filipino dialects, the word has varied positive meanings. Kita can mean income; sight or the ability to see; we or us.

I believe that Kita Corporation is living up to its name. It points the way to other investors as to where they can invest profitably; it has generated income for people on the brink of despair; it has brought the light of life to a place that once was enveloped in darkness and left in desolation. Kita is all that its name implies.

An equally important question: Where

to locate the Aiwa factory.

The obvious choice was LIIP in Binan, Laguna, where we had already purchased eight hectares for future expansion of our manufacturing facilities. Plans were immediately drawn up to design the factory, design the production and materials handling systems, identify contractors to do the job, register a new company and obtain other required permits and approvals.

A ground breaking ceremony was scheduled at LIIP.

Then the phone call came.

Divine intervention, I would call it.

My friend, Tito Henson, President and CEO of Clark Development Corporation (CDC), called me up just days before the scheduled groundbreaking at LIIP for the new factory of Aiwa color TV.

He had heard that we were expanding and thought that by investing in the Clark Special Economic Zone (CSEZ; formerly a major American military base), I could also help the dislocated, jobless, hapless victims of the Mt. Pinatubo eruption, particularly the residents of Pampanga province where Clark was located.

"You pioneered the first industrial estate after the December 1989 coup d'etat," he said, "you may want to invest here in Clark and help our unfortunate residents of Pampanga. I also want you to pioneer here in Clark. We badly need a serious and intrepid investor who will go into manufacturing operations to inspire others to follow."

I postponed the groundbreaking

at LIIP and went to Pampanga with one of my managers, not knowing what to expect.

Stark desolation greeted us. Only the road leading to the CDC offices was swept free of ashfall. Everything else was buried under ashfall dust . . . houses, broken down buildings, debris, ruins all around . . . these were all covered by accumulated dirt since 1991 when Mt. Pinatubo first erupted.

There was evidence that some effort had been exerted to clean up a bit, but the area was just too large to cope with, and the volcanic dust, too much. It seemed a formidable task to clean up. Clark Field was certainly not an attractive place then. It was pitiful.

Tito Henson had sent one of his staff to show us the available spaces for lease. We finally arrived at a spot near the foundation of one crushed building. As I stood there, an inner voice prompted me to say to my manager, "Let us lease this place."

"You are psychic,"

my mother used to tell me. I am inclined to believe her. How else shall I explain my seemingly rash decision to lease a place that looked similar to the deserts of Saudi Arabia? My manager and Tito Henson's man were astounded. I must have sounded daft, but it was as though I glimpsed a vision through all the pall of dust around us. I pointed to all directions . . . east, west, north and south . . . then asked Tito Henson's man how big the area was after the survey.

All of ten hectares, was his reply.

I clearly visualized how our manufacturing company would look like, standing regal in that vast expanse of God-given land. I said as much to my staff involved in the preparation of the Laguna-site groundbreaking. They, too, were astounded and none of them thought it would be possible nor feasible. In fact, almost all of my managers tried to dissuade me but my mind was made up. The company had to be in Clark. To do it, however, I needed the approval of Aiwa.

I needed the approval

of Dr. Susumo Yoshida and Mr. Hajime Unoki, Chairman and President, respectively, of Aiwa Co., Ltd., before I could bring my color TV manufacturing company to Clark.

They were going to be very much involved in the manufacture of our product; they were going to send their logistic personnel and their quality controller; they were to approve local parts for use in production, as well as be involved in a whole year of implementation of manpower. So I met with their representatives to discuss the matter.

As expected, they did not approve

my proposed change of location at our first meeting.

We held many meetings because it was crucial to have absolute agreement. I had to convince them to see things the way I saw them, and in so doing, I took pains to assure them that certain matters could be resolved, such as:

• **Water.** This could be hauled in through water tankers.
• **Electricity.** Electric generator sets could be rented. Both water and electrical power were already being addressed by CDC.
• **Manpower.** The local residents from among whom we would recruit our manpower are intelligent, hardworking, of good attitude, and entrepreneurial in spirit.
• **Housing.** The Aiwa engineers would be staying in the New World Hotel in Makati temporarily until we could find suitable housing near the site. And besides, Mr. Henson promised us some housing units inside Clark which we would renovate quickly for the use of Aiwa engineers.

• **Transportation.** Good brand new cars would be provided for the Aiwa engineers. I mentioned that I was also involved in car manufacturing through Columbian Autocars Corporation and it would be a minimal problem to obtain good cars for this requirement.

• **Communication.** Cellular phones could immediately be provided. Mr. Henson of CDC also promised to provide telephone lines.

• **Amenities.** Other conveniences like relaxation facilities similar to those in Makati, the nation's business center located in Metro Manila, were also available. The Mimosa Resort and Golf Club inside Clark would soon be fully operational.

I also justified the change in site

by telling them that Laguna was already congested with factories. Jobs were already abundant in the area, and the people there did not need us as much as the people of Pampanga.

I also pointed out that should we decide to expand later, the industrial estate at LIIP would not have as much space as Clark had to offer. I also stressed that Clark was offering us the chance to become an active participant in the economic development of a needy place and needy citizens. Clark was a challenge to us. "I believe in the people of Pampanga, and I believe in the future of Clark!" I told them.

Perhaps they got tired of arguing

with a stubborn woman like me. After travelling all the way from Japan several times to try to change my mind and hearing me repeat the same arguments over and over, I finally wore them out. They agreed at last to the change in location — from Laguna to Clark Field in Pampanga — though with apparent feelings of personal discomfort. I was, nonetheless, happy with their nod of approval.

The art of negotiating with the Japanese demands patience and understanding on one's part. The idea is to get their full cooperation by your sincerity and by making good on your word because, in business, your word is equal to your name and vice-versa. Perhaps, I should also add tenacity to one's goals. Had I given up after two meetings, we might not have made it to Clark.

Wrangling over the site

made us lose two months of construction time. But I was informed that the launching of the Aiwa color TV in Japan could not be postponed. It was scheduled for September 1994, or about six months from the time Aiwa finally agreed on the new factory location. More significantly, it was a day that depended on how prompt we would be with our initial shipment; otherwise, there would be no Philippine-made Aiwa color TV to launch.

Owing to the tight schedule, we had to order in advance the production equipment as well as the raw materials needed for production. Now that we had won our Japanese partners' assent to the change in location, it was time for hard work. We worked feverishly to bring to fruition our vision for Clark. New building plans were drawn and I lost no time in getting a contractor to do the job.

"Don't even breathe;

finish the work in six months," was my only instruction to the contractor.

Sure enough, actual work on the site started on April 25, 1994, on a 24-hour, 3-shift basis. The problems we had to surmount would have daunted most people. No water source, no electricity, no drainage, no nothing.

Each time we drove over there, our car was alwav̄

transformed into a running dust-carrier and had to be washed thoroughly upon getting home. Lahar dust, believe me, is rather hard to wash off. It's sticky powder that won't wash off easily. The dust wasn't all that stood in our way; the weather and nature too were not always friendly. Mt. Pinatubo continued to rumble and quake, spewing ashes from time to time and causing lahar to flow nearby. Through sun, dust, wind and storm, however, the construction crew carried on. They lived on site to maximize labor time.

They had a difficult time tearing down one collapsed building because of its sturdy foundation. It stood in the way of the planned new structure, however, so it had to go. It did give way eventually, but only after so many drills had been broken, and so many hands had been severely callused. What about water? They were trucked in by several 250-gallon water tankers daily. The rented generator sets provided all the electricity needed.

Power was intermittently interrupted and so we had our electrician on site to troubleshoot each time an electrical problem arose. To establish contact with our people in Manila, we had to set up our own radio-communication system since even cellular phones were ineffective. There was no let-up on work and no problem was allowed to remain unresolved. Needless to say, the construction of the plant was finished in record time of six months!

I have no words

to describe how I felt, how we all felt, when we prepared the invitations for the opening of the Kita factory. All the problems we had to surmount to make such an event possible made the feeling of accomplishment too sweet for words. Our invitation read:

Kita Corporation
and
Clark Plastic Manufacturing Corporation
request the honour of your presence
at the inauguration of their
Manufacturing Facilities

on Friday, the 24th of November, 1995
at 10 o'clock in the morning
at Clark Special Economic Zone
Clark Field, Pampanga

Our guests and friends came surprised to see our expansive factory building within clean, wholesome, and spacious grounds. There was none of the bleak and desolate spectacle that the volcanic ashfall of erupting Mt. Pinatubo had left. An excellent world class working environment stood in place of the once desert-like mound of lahar dust and pampas grass. We had built a productive facility in a region of our country that had been given up for lost to poverty and despair.

We needed

one month to set up production and at least one month to train production personnel. So, about four months before the estimated completion date of our new consumer electronics factory in Clark, we started to look for qualified people to hire and to train.

There was a lack of skilled electronic technicians, supervisory and managerial personnel in the area. These types of employees were either working as overseas contract workers (OCWs) or were already gainfully employed in Metro Manila. Readily available to us were unskilled high school graduates whom we are currently hiring and training continuously.

I did not mind having to employ unskilled high school graduates because my rationale for building the factory in Clark was to provide livelihood opportunities to the people of Pampanga. It was better for their morale than giving them dole-outs through endless fundraising activities. As the saying goes, give a man fish, and you feed him for a day, but teach him to fish and you feed him for a lifetime. This is the essence of what we are doing in Clark. We are giving the people back their lives and their self-esteem.

So we hired the locals and brought them to our Solid Bulacan factory for training. They were housed in nearby apartments. There, they trained for three months in the production of color TV sets.

Values formation,
in addition to skills training, is a major component of our personnel training.

We instill in them Kita's Corporate Mission:
• To uphold the dignity of the Filipino and to improve the quality and living standards of employees to meet the challenges of the next century.
• For the youth to have the courage, strength, and conviction to strive for excellence by giving their very best in everything they do.
• That the young people of Kita Corporation will contribute to the enhancement of knowledge and values. And for them to share their lives with others by their active involvement in community development and nation-building.

We teach them how to do their best. We ask for commitment, cooperation, and the ability to establish intelligent strategies in the outcome of their work.

By commitment, we mean being focused and dedicated to one's job; it also means being punctual and knowing all there is to know about the job at hand.

Cooperation means being able to get along well with everyone; to be an asset to one another; to help, to improve and be part of a team at work.

Having intelligent strategy means being innovative, creative, and intelligent enough to formulate a plan that will produce the best results from one's work.

We teach our personnel not only to be good but also to be competent.

We discourage our men from unnecessary layering, that is, accomplishing work with too much help from others. While cooperation is a must, the worker must learn to be able to do things on his own when need be.

Over and above these qualities, I expect our men to be imbued with the basic values of decency, fair play, honesty, thrift, concern for others, care and devotion to one's family.

These are the fundamental imprints I want to see in all our officers and employees. Towards these, I try to be a role model. I live with these principles at work, at home, at play, with my family and in the community.

As we continued our preparations

for full-scale production during those first six months, I saw that with all the natural and man-made problems we had to confront, we could not produce our Aiwa color TV at the Clark factory to be able to meet the September 27, 1994, shipout deadline that Aiwa gave us.

Thus, I decided to subcontract the job to SSEC, Inc., one of our other manufacturing companies with a customs bonded warehouse number M1461, in order to meet our export commitment. We sent the 149 people we had hired and trained at our Solid Bulacan factory to the SSEC factory in Balintawak, Quezon City. At SSEC, they would man the production lines to produce the 4,000 sets of Aiwa color TV that were to be our initial shipment to Japan.

However, if the elements gave our laborers so much headache during construction, certain personnel of the Bureau of Customs gave us serious problems during our initial production stage, including having my reputation tarnished by unfounded media reports.

A certain customs man

at the CSEZ customs house was the root of said problems.

All our importations of raw materials and other parts for the manufacture of TV were approved by CDC. During this transition period and by virtue of the subcontracting agreement we had with SSEC, Inc., which was also approved by CDC, these imported raw materials and parts had to be brought over to SSEC's customs bonded warehouse.

The authorizations to bring out the goods from CSEZ to SSEC, Inc.,were approved by CDC through its Vice-President for Business Development and Marketing, Mr. Francis C. Elum. However, the Customs Collector at Clark had consistently delayed his approval of our requests for transfer of parts and components from CSEZ on the ground that he had to obtain authority from his superiors at the Bureau of Customs central office.

It was pretty obvious to us that he had intended to put a monkey-wrench on our export operation for his own personal reasons. Accordingly, in order to address the particular problem posed by the Clark customs man, we obtained authority from the Bureau of Customs central office prior to every transfer of goods. But even if our documents were all complete and in order, the Clark customs man would still manage to delay his approval of our transfer requests by being conveniently absent from or out of his office.

I thought that this particular government functionary had no sense of urgency and gave very little importance to what we were doing to contribute to the country's economy and provide livelihood and employment to the lahar-affected people of Pampanga.

When the ill intentions

of the Clark customs man became clear to us, I complained to his superiors at the Bureau of Customs, namely, Customs Commissioner Guillermo C. Parayno, Jr. and his special assistant, Atty. Adelina Molina, who were receptive to our plight as a fledgling Filipino exporter still trying to make our mark in the global consumer electronics market.

It was clear to us that we could not meet the September 27 deadline of Aiwa, what with the delays we suffered in the transfer of parts and components from CSEZ to SSEC. So, on September 25, 1994, I informed Aiwa Co., Ltd. (Japan), that we could not meet their deadline and requested for an extension. I gathered, however, that all their preparations for the launching of the Aiwa color TV model in Japan were complete and all that they needed were the color TV sets from us.

I had earlier explained the difficulties we were having with our government bureaucracy so that the delay was not a total surprise to them. However, they wanted a firm commitment from me so that they could time their marketing activities accordingly. My General Manager told me that we could ship out our first export of Aiwa color TV by September 29, 1994, since only a few parts needed to be transferred to SSEC to complete our initial production. I relayed this to Aiwa-Japan who agreed to this new schedule.

We immediately filed our transfer requests for the remaining parts and components with the Clark customs house. The production people were able to come out with 665 finished sets of Aiwa color TV by September 26, 1996. We then wrote a request to the Clark customs house for the inspection of these finished units at SSEC customs bonded warehouse and filed our papers to export the same to Japan. Despite our almost hourly follow up, the Clark customs man refused to act on our request for inspection of finished goods for export in total disregard of the endorsement of Atty. Adelina Molina of the Office of the Customs Commissioner and the approval of CDC.

I was again unable to ship out

my goods on September 29. I had to once more explain the matter to Aiwa-Japan and begged them to keep faith with me in the capability and competence of the Filipino.

Aiwa agreed to postpone the launching of their color TV in Japan for the second time. However, they informed me that the final shipout deadline was October 5; otherwise, I had to send them at least one container by air at my own expense. This would be a significant cost to me. But I knew that the more damaging result of our inability to meet our export deadline would be the cancellation of our purchase agreement. That would be a devastating loss, not only to me personally but to the country as well. Imagine the jobs and the foreign exchange revenues that would be lost as well as the opportunity to learn new technology in consumer electronics manufacturing!

On September 28, 1994, I again wrote Customs Commissioner Parayno complaining of the inaction of the Clark customs man which had resulted in our inability to export finished color TV sets to Aiwa Co. Ltd.. I cited to him the damage and injury done by this customs person on our country's economic program. I also wrote Secretary Roy Navarro of the Department of Trade and Industry reporting my problem in exporting goods manufactured in the Philippines.

This was probably the proverbial straw that broke the camel's back. Commissioner Parayno recalled his man at Clark and replaced him with a professional, Collector Antonio Marquez. With a new customs man at Clark, I was finally able to make my first export of 1,995 sets of Aiwa color TV in three 40-foot containers on October 5, 1994.

But that was not the end

of my troubles with the former Clark customs man.

He sent letters to the President of the Philippines, to certain senators and members of Congress accusing me of smuggling out of the CSEZ. He even included me as a principal together with Commissioner Guillermo Parayno and Atty. Adelina Molina of the Bureau of Customs and Mr. Antonio Henson and Mr. Francis Elum of the CDC in a case he filed before the Ombudsman.

One senator, using the distorted information provided by the former Clark customs man, delivered a privilege speech in the halls of the Philippine Senate exposing what he alleged was smuggling at Clark and the existence of a syndicate which he called the "Clark Connection." The senator named me and my company in Clark , among others, as being involved in this alleged activity. Without getting our side of the issue, media played up the "exposé" of this senator.

But my faith in the goodness of the Filipino was further strengthened when Customs Commissioner Guillermo C. Parayno, Jr., and CDC President and CEO Tito Henson, in a press conference, belied any smuggling activity in Clark nor my involvement in one.

I also wrote a letter to then Senate President Edgardo Angara, protesting strongly against the allegation that I or my company in Clark were involved in a smuggling syndicate called the "Clark Connection."

I asked that an investigation be made by the entire Philippine Senate of the smuggling charges leveled against me by one of their members so that the truth would be heard.

I also asked him whether the Senate's Ethics Committee could provide some relief to ordinary citizens who are willfully and maliciously harassed by any member of the Senate hiding behind parliamentary immunity.

I disclosed as much of my anguish as I could in my letter to Sen. President Angara, specifically telling him of the damage and injury wrought on our export operation at Clark; how, because of the chain of events, our foreign buyers expressed doubts on our ability as a country to compete for business with other countries. The bad publicity caused by all the hullabaloo prompted interested investors to question the sanity of investing in our country.

Media had a field day

playing up the controversy. "Is she . . . or isn't she . . . a smuggler" was the popular theme of the daily newspapers and TV newscasters, as well as radio talebearers.

There were those who objectively reported the news and affirmed their trust in me and in our firm. There were also those who used the unfortunate incident to justify throwing mud at me and my company in Clark.

Not wanting to be outdone,

the Congressional Ad Hoc Oversight Committee on Bases Conversion, in what to me was another .case of political grandstanding, also invited me and my Clark company to a so-called "public hearing in aid of legislation." It was to be held on December 6, 1994, which was long after we had made our first export of Aiwa color TV sets to Japan. They said they wanted to investigate the supposed controversy involving duty-free stores and including alleged smuggling activities.

In a position paper I submitted to the Committee, I denied any involvement in any smuggling activity pointing out the fact that the color TV I was producing in Clark was Japanese NTSC which had no local market and that the same issue had been discredited by the Bureau of Customs and the Clark Development Corporation.

I mentioned the contributions being made by my Clark company to the local and national economy specifically in terms of job and livelihood generation and foreign exchange receipts.

I also brought attention to the fact that unfounded and malicious charges made by any member of the legislature against legitimate businesses negatively affect the country as an investment destination.

Finally, I put the Committee to task with the following expectations:

1. Come out with a resolution to be made available to the public clearly stating the results of the public hearing.

2. Pass a resolution as basis for legislation to prevent the abuse of parliamentary immunity and protect the rights of private citizens from undue harassment by any member of Congress.

3. Propose legislation that would effectively curb the damaging activities of public officials who do not render good public service.

4. Propose improvements in existing trade transaction procedures to facilitate the promotion of exports and reduce bureaucratic red tape.

Up to this time, I haven't heard from the Senate or from the House of Representatives as to the results of their investigations or inquiries "in aid of legislation."

I was, nonetheless, encouraged

by the private sector's show of support for my fight to right a wrong.

The Philippine Chamber of Commerce and Industry (PCCI) issued a strong statement to media on December 8, 1994, denouncing the abuse of privilege speech by legislators who are protected by legal immunity.

Similarly, the Employers Confederation of the Philippines (ECOP) passed a board resolution on December 9, 1994, supporting my demand for investigation of the charges aired against me in the Senate, asking for legislation that would set guidelines in the observance of parliamentary immunity, and appealing to the Senate to observe parliamentary propriety and decorum in airing accusations against private citizens.

There were many others in the private sector who expressed similar sentiments. Thus, I knew that I had sent a strong message and that the real Filipino would not allow injustice to go unnoticed.

Painful experience? It is not

something to look forward to, but it is something the entrepreneur must learn to expect. People will find it easier to believe bad things said about you than any good thing that may be said of you. But one must persevere and stand by one's principles.

After my difficult experience in making my first export of Aiwa color TV, I thought that it would be smooth sailing after that. The Bureau of.Customs under the leadership of Commissioner Guillermo Parayno, Jr., and the CDC under its President, Tito Henson, were fully supportive of our export operations from Clark.

Because of a number of issues which I brought up to the attention of Tito Henson while he was still President of CDC, I felt some regret when he left CDC. While there had been some agreements, these issues were still to be conclusively resolved at the time he stepped down.

When the new CEO of CDC assumed office, I sent him a letter to remind him of the issues which I had earlier taken up with his predecessor. The more significant of these were:

1. Straight lease of 50 years on land occupied by my Clark manufacturing company.

CDC had earlier informed me that the law governing the operation of CDC did not allow lease agreements to exceed 25 years, renewable for the same period.

However, I learned that another company located inside the CSEZ had been given a 50 years straight lease with renewal option for another 25 years. CDC informed me that the 50 year straight lease was given only to foreign firms and not to Filipinos, in accordance with the guidelines of the BOI.

I was surprised at this piece of information. It made me feel like a second-class citizen in my own country.

On May 16, 1996, I wrote BOI Governor Ofelia V. Bulaong asking for clarification on the BOI guidelines referred to by CDC which I strongly felt were anti-Filipino.

The BOI acted swiftly and judiciously and wrote CDC to favorably endorse our request for a fifty-year lease. The BOI also further clarified that while CDC was correct to interpret the law in favor of foreigners, the law was not intended to discriminate against Filipinos. At this time we are awaiting CDC's favorable response considering that the legal impediment cited has been clarified by the BOI.

2. Lease of four clusters of housing units inside CSEZ.

These housing units were intended for use by Aiwa engineers and our senior managers.

The previous CDC Board of Directors approved our request but implementation was delayed as we were trying to negotiate for better terms since we would do the renovation ourselves.

However, the new CDC management informed me that the housing units would no longer be leased out based on the previous CDC approval. Instead, CDC would renovate and develop these housing units to be later on leased at very much higher rates.

This change disappointed me because of the seeming lack of consistency and continuity in decision making. However, I am still hopeful that we can still revert to the original agreements once the new management is apprised of the facts.

3. Lease of additional land area (approximately two hectares) adjoining our leased property.

This matter was approved by the previous CDC management although the contract was not written up in time. The new CDC management, after several months of follow-up, finally prepared the contract but the rental rate was higher than what was originally approved.

I also wrote several letters to the Chairman of the Bases Conversion Development Authority (and concurrent Chairman of CDC), regarding the foregoing cases involving my operations at Clark.

The changes in key personnel apparently

affected the early resolution of our requests because, surely, any new manager must take time to learn the ropes, so to speak.

We understand that matters as serious as the ones we were trying to work out with the CDC require careful analysis and study. In our urgent desire to resolve major items, such as revision of the lease term, the lease of housing units, and request for additional space, we painstakingly justified our cause by citing our investment figures and the fact that we accounted for almost 70 per cent of total export revenues of Clark.

Our discussions with CDC's previous management covered significant ground and we assumed that the paper work was a matter of course. We also trusted that the commitments we concluded would be binding on succeeding administrations.

While there is no indication that these tentative agreements will be summarily rescinded, over a year after we first presented our intentions, we are still awaiting significant developments with respect to our requests, favorable or otherwise.

It is almost axiomatic for any investor to expect, at the very least, prompt attention on matters such as long-term leases which could very well have a major impact on capital investment decisions. While we have been zealous in our desire to contribute to the development of an economically ravaged area such as Clark, we likewise have a commitment to our other stakeholders to take care of our return-on investment (ROI).

Then with hardly any consultation

with affected parties, the new management of CDC decided to raise additional revenues for its operations by increasing the fees imposed on CSEZ investors.

On January 24, 1996, CDC announced a new schedule of fees to be imposed effective February 1, 1996, on all the businesses operating inside the CSEZ.

Most investors found the fees unreasonable, if not downright improper considering that CDC was supposed to serve the Clark investors whom they practically begged to set up shop inside the terribly devastated CSEZ in the aftermath of the Mt. Pinatubo eruption.

These fees included:

1. The sale of accountable forms (to be used in almost every transaction done inside the CSEZ), "at cost plus 100% mark-up."

2. Fines and penalties for the non-submission of periodic reports at "P1,000.00 for the first day of delay plus an addition of P100.00 per day of delay, and pending of all requests until payment is made."

A delayed report could mean that goods, whether incoming, outgoing, or within the Special Economic Zone, will not move. That would certainly result in tremendous losses and, for an exporter like me, the loss of my export market, my credibility and reliability as supplier of goods, and my competitiveness.

This new imposition by CDC galvanized most of the Clark investors into action.

Because of my huge investment in Clark and my good export performance with my Aiwa color TV and because I don't allow injustice to be done, I agreed to the request of the Clark investors for me to spearhead the movement to oppose the new fees.

To unify the Clark investors into an organization that would have significant voice in negotiating with CDC, I proposed the setting up of an investors' association under a corporate structure. Thus was the Clark Investors and Locators Association (CILA), Inc., born. The association then passed a resolution opposing the new CDC fee structure because it:

1. "Defeats the very cornerstone of the CSEZ which seeks to develop the air base, constantly threatened by lahar and ashfall, into a hub of economic activities that would attract foreign and local investors to situate their factories/operations/services in the CSEZ;

2. "Runs counter to the government thrust of providing jobs to the many displaced and unemployed work force in the region;

3. "Is contrary to the government's policy of promoting exports as the linchpin of the country's economic development;

4. "Provides barriers to the quest of the people for an improved quality of life through enhancement of skills and employment; and

5. "Reduces the competitiveness of Philippine-made products and services through additional costs and bureaucratic procedures that result in delays."

The new CDC management showed magnanimity in its response by suspending the implementation of the new schedule of fees and tariffs until full consultation with the Clark investors was made. Up to this time, the implementation of the new fees is still suspended and dialogues and consultations are being made between the Clark investors and CDC management. I am happy that I contributed to the empowerment of the investors and locators in Clark.

In spite of all these, we have not lost our confidence in the current management of CDC. It has shown on several other occasions the willingness to listen, act decisively, and be sensitive to the interests of the investors. We anticipate that it will be fully capable of understanding the predicament of all those who decided to invest in Clark.

We do not, however, expect to see the last of our problems. I am afraid that somewhere along the way, an overzealous bureaucrat may again come up with the next bright idea on how to make things a little more difficult.

We thank God that for every one of them, there are also countless others who invariably have a genuine feel for the enterprising spirit. There is no doubt about the help these wondrous souls in government have extended to us. I will forever cherish them in my memories for understanding their role in nation building.

If I have been too candid in my observations which may seem a bit bold and frank to others, I apologize.

As if all the problems
were not enough, we got another disappointing shock when, in early June, 1996, we received a claim from our major export customer for 329 TV sets which were reported missing.

Our investigation disclosed another clear and present threat to our credibility as a major global trader. The TV sets were not short-shipped. They were simply hijacked on the way to the pier after the container left Clark. Our own investigation showed indications of the existence of a syndicate which preys on shipments of high-value merchandise in transit to the loading docks.

Such a situation is most embarrassing

for both exporters and government because it creates doubts on our collective capability to protect property. We wrote concerned government officials, including the President, to make them aware of this potent danger to our export industry. We urged them to take immediate steps to prevent similar occurrences which will make our buyers lose confidence in our capability to export efficiently according to their confirmed orders.

The government officials reacted quickly, and recovered 47 units in a warehouse somewhere in Dagat-dagatan, Manila, with more arrests and recoveries expected. We appreciate the quick action which is a strong deterrent to future hijackings and we were happy to report to our buyer that the incident was properly and quickly attended to. This was one instance where swift, and encouraging government action reinforces one's belief that with determination, cooperation, and concerted effort, the results could be remarkably outstanding.

Today, Kita Corporation

is primarily engaged in the manufacture of consumer electronic products for export, as a registered enterprise in the Clark Special Economic Zone. As such, it is entitled to tax and duty free importations of capital equipment, raw materials and supplies.

As a manufacturer of consumer electronic products, Kita Corporation imports raw materials, parts and supplies. It also buys local parts and supplies like packaging materials subject to quality approval by our foreign buyers who own the brand names as well as the product designs.

The initial product being manufactured by Kita Corporation is the Aiwa brand of color TV for export to Japan. This product is designed to function under the Japanese standard NTSC broadcast signal system and, therefore, has no local market. The Philippines uses NTSC standard which is American NTSC standard that is different from that used in Japan. Eventually, Kita will produce Aiwa color TV with American NTSC standard.

The cost of building the factory was more than P100 million. Most of the personnel are Pampangueños, residents of Angeles, Pampanga, where Clark Field is situated.

The prestigious JQA

Product Safety Certification has been awarded to Kita Corporation.

"JQA" stands for "Japan Quality Assurance" Organization, a private institution affiliated with the Japanese government.

It is one of the most prestigious and credible international bodies engaged in testing the safety of electrical products. It also confirms the quality assurance system of the factory concerned, and gives a certificate to each product. Only products certified by JQA can bear the JQA safety certification mark.

In June 1996, a JQA inspection team visited Kita's Clark factory to review its quality and safety standards and practices. Based on the inspection, the team recommended the award to Kita of the JQA certification, attesting to Kita's high quality standards. Kita is the first such Philippine company in the consumer electronics business to be awarded the JQA certificate.

The total exports

made by industrial firms located inside the Clark Special Economic Zone for the first quarter of 1996 reached US$30.47 million. The leading newspapers reported this information, and one newspaper then ran on to say:

"Kita Corporation, a Filipino-owned electronics firm, again emerged as the top exporter among investor-companies at Clark Field. It posted US$20.58 million or 68% of the total exports from Clark for the first quarter. Kita, which assembles television sets for the Japan-based Aiwa Ltd. Corp., also has export markets in the Middle East and Europe."

As of May 16, 1996, Kita Corporation has exported a total of 559,939 units of Aiwa color TV with sales value of US$89.37 million.

I feel very happy that my efforts to promote the competence, capability and integrity of the Filipino is bearing fruit in the global market. But I only know very well that the fight is not yet won.

In 1997, we will be exporting at least a million Aiwa color TV sets. But already we are planning to prepare for our audio export project also with Aiwa Co., Ltd.. We are preparing ourselves to expand our activities into components manufacturing such as speakers, printed circuit boards, and the like.

This is not where dreams end.

A lot of work remains to be done to bring economic independence to many Filipinos. Those of us who have the ability and capacity to contribute towards this end must do so. There are no barriers but ourselves (except those coming from God or from nature which are beyond our control).

While we cannot fight against God and Nature, we must take a stand and summon all our courage to fight against needless bureaucracy. I sincerely believe that there are many good men in the government service. It is a matter of working more closely with them and, in a spirit of cooperation and transparency, come up with less obstructions to doing business.

Through Kita, we have invested more than P700 million in Clark, but our greater investment is in our people, specifically the residents of Pampanga, by hiring them and infusing life once again into their lahar-devastated community. We have also placed the Philippines on the map . . . the global market map by catering to the communication needs of the sophisticated markets of Japan, Europe, and Saudi Arabia.

Kita Corporation is a monument to the indomitable spirit of the Filipino, a testament to the resiliency of our people to rise from disaster and despondency to greater challenge and productivity.

I am glad Kita is playing a great part in the transformation of our people.

AFTERTHOUGHT

I have been blessed in countless ways.

Of all that came my way, and next to my family of course, nothing gives me more satisfaction and fulfillment than to have been able to enjoy the kind of self-expression to pursue every worthwhile opportunity, explore possibilities, speak out with a passion on issues I cared about, and manage people and resources.

The greatest good for the greatest number has always been my guiding light. There were times when mine was a voice in the wilderness, when the numbers didn't add up, and all the experts said otherwise.

In many instances, I found the courage to take what the poet Robert Frost called the "road least travelled by," and indeed, "it has made all the difference." I thank God for this occasional foolhardiness. But then again, each one of us can be capable of great vision and courage in the midst of adversity.

The anecdotes, stories, and experiences I just shared with you could very well happen to countless other Elenas. I am sure there is a somebody who was, is, and will be, in similar situations.

How we respond to challenges is a product of our fundamental beliefs, values, and faith. Almost always we need an overdose of common sense. We could also try keeping our feet on the ground while putting our heads above the clouds, that is, keeping track of the basics while allowing the mind to wander in search of the imponderables.

In all my years, I have been inspired by a few

simple, albeit fundamental, precepts which have guided my relationship with God and my fellowmen. My experiences, no matter how inconsequential or unhappy, have not shaken these beliefs a single bit. They have only gotten stronger over the years. I have also discovered, validated, and am now living by, certain principles which have only reinforced my basic trust in the goodness of persons.

I have always known and believed absolutely that there is only one freedom given to man by God. It is the freedom to do good. What you say and do is your choice but this choice cannot supersede the freedom to do good.

I also go by the following principles:

Believe in yourself. If you don't, you cannot believe in your country and people.

Serve family and country for the glory of God.

Standard of living is important, but standard of being is more important.

Look at money and possessions not as your personal ownership. You are simply a trustee morally tasked with the responsibility to create wealth and benefits for the good of many. I always remember that in a few years, my possessions will be totally irrelevant to me but the good done will continue to help many people, the heritage left will still be affecting the lives of many.

Be a good trustee. Generate savings to benefit others. Self-indulgence is a sign of stoic pride.

Adopt a work ethic that will bring dignity and pride to yourself, your family, and your neighbor. Work is the most powerful prayer and the source of all welfare.

Help as many persons as you can and harm no one. This itself is service to people. I can endure injury to my person, but when injury hurts the lives of many others, have the courage to fight it.

Courtesy extended to superiors is called appropriate decorum; if extended among equals, it is civility; but courtesy extended to subordinates is nobility.

Leadership by example is a universal truth. Leading by example is what counts. The only way. It is everything.

Have a vision. Pursue it with passion and honor.

These tenets have guided me every day of my life and surely there were times when even these fundamental beliefs were challenged, not because of faith wavering, but because of events, circumstances, threats, opportunities, and challenges inherently present in the often rough and tumble world of business. It is not unusual to find yourself alone with your beliefs.

The challenge is in keeping the faith and maintaining your perspective, dignity, honor, and humor in the midst of uncertainty and trepidation.

I hope I have succeeded in touching the entrepreneurial spirit in you. It is also my fervent wish that people would take the initial steps towards realizing their potentials by first reaching within themselves to discover their motivations, fears, dreams, hopes, aspirations, values, and beliefs. For a prospective entrepreneur, these are the ingredients that make a potent brew if kindled with enough fire and fanned by an indomitable spirit to succeed.

My story should not only inspire but should pose a challenge to everyone. I cannot be alone. There are enough challenges and opportunities for everybody.

If my stories could swing a lesson or two on how to do business in the real world . . . how to make money without losing your soul . . . if they can make the reader a little more aware, take one less step, clinch one more deal, create one more job, and just a little bit more of everything, then we've all done it our way.

www.ingramcontent.com/pod-product-compliance
Lightning Source LLC
Chambersburg PA
CBHW071403170526
45165CB00001B/159